THE LUNATIC FRINGE

•

The mere example of non-conformity is itself a service. Precisely because the tyranny of opinion is such as to make eccentricity a reproach, it is desirable, in order to break through that tyranny, that people should be eccentric.

——JOHN STUART MILL

•

Nescis, mi fili, quantilla sapientia regitur mundus.

——POPE JULIUS III

•

In a nation of one hundred fine, mob-hearted,
 relenting, repenting millions,
There are plenty of sweeping, swinging, stinging,
 gorgeous things to shout about,
And knock your old blue devils out.

——VACHEL LINDSAY

•

THE
LUNATIC
FRINGE

BY

GERALD W. JOHNSON

Philadelphia

J. B. LIPPINCOTT COMPANY

New York

DEDICATED TO THE UNTERRIFIED AMERICAN

IF ANY

CONTENTS

CONTENTS

1

AS YOU LIKE IT

prelude, preamble, preface or apology

YOU AND I, heartily agreeing that we are men of sense, can afford to view the antics of the addlepated with an indulgent eye; but others are not so fortunate. In this midsection of the twentieth century those others—excluding you and me, naturally—are in a state not far removed from the pitiable. They seem to have been converted by the Communist Chinese to the curious cult of the dirty brain and the implied possibility of washing it; and hag-ridden by some inexplicable sense of guilt, they stand in mortal terror of being washed.

You and I, of course, are obsessed by no such nonsense, but as long as our neighbors are, we have to deal with it. Dealing with any form of mental aberration is a difficult op-

eration in which anything that may be of the slightest assistance should be welcomed even by the most skillful. Perhaps
the tales in this volume, all drawn from American history,
may furnish some assistance; it is in that hope that they are
offered.

It is true that the lives of some of these characters present
elements of high comedy, and nearly all afford occasion for
sardonic amusement. So what? If reading the record of the
past provokes an occasional grin, or even a guffaw, it loses
nothing in interest thereby. On the other hand, sometimes
through a rift in the drab texture of the story an unexpected
splendor shines. Again, so what? To learn that Pantaloon
may have had his moments of grace and dignity, to discover
that nobility once inhabited Main Street detracts no whit
from the lure of the quest. But these are by the way, these
are serendipity, these are not the storied unicorn that can
alleviate our woes. That can be attained only if one finds in
these narratives an influence tending to abate to some extent what Dean Griswold calls "the fear around us."

Do not expect to find any rational explanation of the state
of mind that afflicts so many of those among us. The thing
can be defined readily, but a definition is not an explanation.
The definition obviously is the age-old and world-wide fear
of taking the next step; but why this fear should exist, and
why it should be nearly universal, is a mystery that has baffled
all philosophy and certainly will not be explained in this
work.

However, it is not at all difficult to understand why this
fear should have acquired an unexampled malignancy among
Americans as the twentieth century passed into its second
half. A sharp acceleration in the rate of change in all conditions of civilized existence is the most conspicuous characteristic of this century. Whether the trend of change is in

the direction of the improvement or of the deterioration of civilization is immaterial, for the moment; it is sufficient to say that it is rapid.

When change is rapid the number of next steps to be taken is multiplied and the terror of those who fear the next step is correspondingly augmented. So we have presented to our eyes the curious phenomenon of a people, to wit, citizens of the United States of America, who, having destroyed all their armed enemies, having participated, in a single generation, in the overthrow of seven great empires, having gained wealth beyond the wildest dream of Croesus, or of Midas of the golden touch, having raised armies that employ merely as the moving flank as great a force as Napoleon ever commanded, having covered the seas with its fleets and darkened the sky with its flights of bombers, having established powerful garrisons at every strategic point the wide world over—this people is now beset with such fears as it never experienced when Early's Confederate cavalry on the hills of Maryland stared at the spires of Washington, or when the Pacific fleet was wrecked by the enemy in its own harbor.

You and I know better, of course, but it seems to be a fact that those others, our neighbors, look to the survival of the republic with more misgivings than ever troubled Thomas Jefferson or Alexander Hamilton. This, as Grover Cleveland remarked in another connection, is a condition and not a theory, and as a condition it must be faced.

Facing it is the more difficult because the thing itself is faceless. The fact of the prevailing terror is glaringly plain to the dullest, but just what it is that we are afraid of is not easy to make out. We fear the Red army, of course, but that is a rational and limited fear. The Red army is big and very tough; but we have met others that, relatively to our own strength, were bigger and tougher and we have handled them all right. I believe most of those hereinbeforementioned others, while they have no wish to tangle with the Red army, are confident that we can handle it if we must. It is not there that their confidence fails.

The really appalling thing is not the Red army but the fact that, as we are now in a position of leadership it is incumbent upon this nation and no other to take the next step. Our paralyzing fear is fear that it will be a mis-step, and if that occurs it will not be through the machinations of our enemies but through some failure within. Wisdom may fail us, or skill, or perhaps even integrity. Suspicion of everything new and untried and distrust of most things that have been tried, is the prevalent mood, betraying us into such erratic action as the election of last November, when we stampeded into the sheltering arms of the Great White Father while at the same time repudiating the party that he represents. An astonished world could only read the verdict as, "We like Ike, but only with his hands tied," and if the world failed to make sense of it, is it any wonder?

As for you and me, our function is obviously to do what can be done toward reducing this fear to some semblance of rationality. The first step in that direction would seem to be to examine it carefully to make sure that we are not being terrorized by dragons composed of sawdust and papier-mâché. If the fears of our neighbors are not centered upon some foreign foe, then the investigation must turn inward toward the suspected elements of weakness within our gates.

The average American, I believe, now recognizes the new position of the United States in relation to the rest of the world and is of two minds about it. He may not understand at all clearly how we acquired leadership, and he may be somewhat resentful of having it thrust upon us; but at the same time he regards leadership as a position of honor and takes pride in it. On the whole, therefore, he is not unwilling to have this country discharge the function of a leader, but he is gnawed by a remorseless fear that the function may be intrusted to the wrong hands.

That is to say, there is ever present in his mind the possibility, not that we shall be invaded and conquered by the Russians or anyone else, but that the Lunatic Fringe among the native-born may gain control. That is a fear so completely shattering that it gravely impairs his capacity to act as a rational human being.

To combat it is difficult, to eliminate it flatly impossible; but surely it is not unreasonable to hope that it may be reduced to manageable proportions if you and I, being, as we agreed, men of sense, attack it with every weapon that comes to hand. One of these is reasoning by analogy, admittedly an unreliable method but by no means always ineffective. If experience has shown that the Lunatic Fringe of the past has not been as altogether dreadful in either its aims or its accomplishments as the Lunatic Fringe of the present seems to be, perhaps those others may be persuaded to reduce their fears at least far enough to listen to the voice of reason.

To that end there have been assembled here certain tales that are, like Poe's, "of the grotesque and the arabesque," but that nevertheless are taken from familiar sources, acknowledged as authoritative by conservative historians. They are arranged in roughly, but not precisely, chronological sequence; and the latest of them is set far enough in the past to enable the narrator to be reasonably sure that we know how it all came out. One exception to the regular order is the story that leads off, placed at the beginning for reasons that it is hoped will be obvious to the reader.

In dealing with the Lunatic Fringe, then, let us begin with the tale of:

2

THEODORE ROOSEVELT

who coined the phrase

THEODORE ROOSEVELT, one of the great phrase-makers of American public life, in reviewing his own career wrote,

> Then, among the wise and high-minded people who in self-respecting and genuine fashion strive earnestly for peace, there are the foolish fanatics always to be found in such a movement and always discrediting it—the men who form the lunatic fringe in all reform movements.*

Roosevelt the Furious—always to be distinguished from Roosevelt the Miraculous, biologically related to the Furious, but intellectually not in the same phylum, much less the same species—regarded himself as a reformer, and even his non-admirers admitted that he was a deformer or a conformer, forever in the midst of some movement; so his patent annoyance with the Lunatic Fringe requires no explanation. No man cherishes affection for those who discredit him.

He employed the phrase variously. In 1913 it appeared in a speech leveled at the Progressive party, which Roosevelt a year before had led in a campaign that assured the election of a Democrat. In the passage quoted it is directed at people who believed that general disarmament would be a contribution to permanent peace, and its author felt that it carried the weight of an utterance *ex cathedra*, for Roosevelt re-

---

* Roosevelt, Theodore, *Autobiography,* p. 225 (1913 edition)

garded himself as something of a specialist on peace. He had been awarded the Nobel Peace Prize in 1906, and if that did not establish him as an authority on the subject, what could? There were, of course, the ribald who asserted that, like the Englishman who yielded to none in his respect for religion provided it did not interfere with a man's private life, Roosevelt was always in favor of peace provided it did not interfere with the fighting. But such critics were never distinguished by his serious attention, so perhaps we may brush them aside, too.

Yet man, bedeviled by contrarieties in his own nature, long ago learned that he tends to develop a resemblance to what he loves; and Americans of late, through their experience with Communism, have received the horrifying revelation that we tend to become like what we hate, if we hate it intensely enough. So it is not beyond all reason to speculate on the possibility that Roosevelt's frenetic hatred of the Lunatic Fringe may indicate that he had a prominent place therein.

The fact that his admirers gave him the rank of a major prophet in his own day—and some even yet—is irrelevant. Nothing is more certain than the mournful fact that the Socrates of yesterday is frequently the Silly Billy of today. The Roosevelt of 1909, the year of his retirement from the Presidency, is not our concern; it is his appearance in the light of 1957 that should command the attention of the contemporary generation. That his appearance has altered in the course of nearly fifty years goes without saying; but the direction and extent of the alteration may be open to debate.

The inquiry starts with a firm base on one fact so solid that it goes unquestioned in any quarter, to wit, the fact that Theodore Roosevelt was a sensational President. In the long stretch from Abraham Lincoln to Woodrow Wilson, no other President startled the natives with the persistency and success of this one. Some, perhaps, would go further, setting aside

Lincoln and Wilson and averring that for the production of sheer astonishments—not necessarily significances—this President was surpassed only by Andrew Jackson before him and by his cousin, the Miraculous, after him.

There is much to be said for the theory of those who hold that Theodore Roosevelt rescued the Presidency from what Grover Cleveland, with his flair for words that dazed the proletariat, called "innocuous desuetude." Old Andrew Johnson, like Truman, had the weight of the moon and the planets fall on him when Lincoln died; but he had neither Truman's luck nor his political adroitness. He was crushed. Nevertheless, he was a personality; as brave as he was stubborn, while he lasted he maintained the Presidency as the center of national interest.

But the beating he took appalled his successors. For the next thirty years the first objective of the man in the White House was to avoid incurring the devastating wrath of Congress. If Cleveland was forced into doing so, it was to avoid incurring the even more fearsome wrath of "sound men" in the party and in the country. For the rest, the list of Presidents in that period—Grant, Hayes, Garfield, Arthur, Harrison and McKinley—can be matched for feebleness and obscurity only by the list between Polk and Lincoln—Taylor, Fillmore, Pierce and Buchanan. By 1901 the Presidency of the United States had sunk to a level of impotence and inanity comparable to the Presidency of France, or the Presidency of the Union of Soviet Socialist Republics.

T. R. transformed it. Concerning that, there is no disputing. Even those who detested him most heartily could not deny that while he inhabited it the White House was the center of things. It was a storm center, if you please, but it was the center, and Capitol Hill spun to its impulses as helplessly as a yo-yo with an expert handler at the other end of the string.

Naturally, Congress did not like it. Congress never likes to see a President seize the center of the stage, and when one not only seizes it but holds it continuously for seven years the wrath of Congress becomes Olympian. In the reign of Theodore the rage of the Solons was all the hotter for being mixed with an element of astonishment; for thirty years no President had insisted on being the head of the party as well as the head of the state, and Congress had assumed that its dominance was established on a permanent basis. As a matter of course the man who upset it was charged with usurpation of unconstitutional powers, but he was not guilty. He didn't have to be guilty, for the Presidency, as Woodrow Wilson pointed out, is constitutionally as big as the ability of the President can make it.

To do the Republican politicians justice, they had foreseen the possibility of this development and had taken what they believed to be adequate measures to prevent it. When the increase of Theodore's influence as Governor of New York began to reach what they considered monstrous proportions they applied to him what had been up to that time the most effective method of political euthanasia—they embalmed him in the Vice Presidency. It was a smart move, for few who entered that sepulchre were ever heard of again, but it was defeated by the unpredictable act of a madman who killed President McKinley and, as Mark Hanna remarked on the funeral train, "that damned cowboy" was President of the United States by the very act that was intended to keep him out of the White House.

Yet who knows? He might have arrived some other way, and if not, then some other man would certainly have reconstituted the Presidency, for the nation could not have continued much longer under such vacuous leadership as it had had since Johnson.

Theodore Roosevelt was a good man for the job for reasons not all based on his personality. Little attention has been directed to the fact, but we are developing in this country certain great political families comparable to Cecil, Cavendish and Russell in England. Adams comes to mind at once, but Taft is almost as potent now, and Harrison and Stevenson are both good political names. Of all such dynasties, however, the most successful is Roosevelt, for it alone works both sides of the street—its two most brilliant leaders belonged to opposite parties, so no matter whether Democrats or Republicans rule the land some Roosevelt will always be close to the seat of power. In a time of crisis, when radical change is inevitable, there is much to be said for having at the center of power one who is by inheritance and training committed to preserving as much of the old as can be preserved—that is to say, an aristocrat.

Perhaps every Roosevelt, certainly including the two most famous, Theodore and Franklin, should, like those uncommon emperors of Byzantium who came to the throne by legitimate succession to their fathers, have added to his own name *Porphyrogenitus,* "born in the purple," for he starts life with an advantage not, perhaps, as great, but as definite as that of boys born in the porphyry-tiled maternity ward of the Byzantine imperial palace. The family is ancient, as American families go, and has transmitted its inheritance both of wealth and of intelligence remarkably well. True, neither its riches nor its scholarship have ever been superlative, but they have always been sufficient to enable its leaders to be active in the field of public affairs unhandicapped by either poverty or ignorance.

Yet it would seem that the Roosevelt blood requires some kind of sting to set it racing at the most effective speed. Theodore and Franklin were both physically handicapped, one by asthma in childhood, the other by polio in early manhood, and it is easy to believe that the force that each developed in maturity was what the psychologists call over-compensation and Toynbee calls successful response to a challenge.

Certainly the nightmare that haunted the asthmatic young Theodore was dread of developing into a moral and physical weakling, and he reacted to it with great violence. No medieval ascetic intent upon mortification of the flesh held to his regimen more rigorously than Theodore Roosevelt held to the exercises that he thought would toughen and invigorate the flesh. Today some medical opinion holds that he overdid it; for he died at less than sixty-one and his physical breakdown is traced to a too-strenuous exploration in the South American jungles.

Whatever the reason, he came to manhood with a tremendous, a morbid appetite for the experience of the common man. He was not a common man; he was decidedly uncommon, and he knew it; but he was eaten by the fear that his departure from the norm might be below rather than above it, particularly in the matter of physical strength and endurance. So he boxed, wrestled, swam and rode incessantly; in 1884 he adopted the life of a cattleman on the Western plains, undoubtedly because the popular fancy regarded it as the extreme of hardihood at the time. But when he almost lost his shirt, financially, by his ranching adventure, common sense reasserted itself and he returned to New York, although he continued his indulgence in violent exercise.

All this fascinated the public to such an extent that little attention was paid to the fact that Roosevelt's frantic desire was to share not merely the labors and sports of the average American, but also his thoughts and aspirations. A scion of the old Roosevelt family of New York and through his mother a descendant of the president of the first Provincial Congress of Georgia, educated first by tutors and then becoming a Phi Beta Kappa of Harvard, heir to a comfortable fortune, he was not and could not possibly be an average

American. But he never ceased trying, and the effort gave a touch of the synthetic, the not-quite-genuine to his whole career.

Yet it was not a discreditable effort. Theodore Roosevelt was conscientiously practicing what he sincerely believed to be democracy, and if he fell into error it was an intellectual, not a moral error. He was filled with a perfectly genuine loathing of the snobbery that endeavored to erect wealth into a patent of nobility; and if his detestation of that sort of thing drove him into an inverted snobbery, the detestation, at least, was credible. The truth is he was not quite the complete aristocrat—not a Washington, or a Jefferson who could sympathize with and wholeheartedly admire the common man without ever attempting or desiring to identify himself with the proletarian. His cousin had that trick to perfection, but Theodore never mastered it.

Nevertheless, from the practical standpoint his success was remarkable. He was essentially a scholar driven by his fear of weakness to become an athlete not merely in the physical but also in the intellectual realm. He wrote a great deal and, within limits, he wrote well; but every book he turned out was what rhetoricians term an agon, an effort to establish a point, to correct a misconception, to demolish an error—in short, a struggle, if not against an opponent in flesh and blood, then against a maleficent idea, always the pitting of his strength and skill against an antagonist. Neither the calmly reflective mood nor daring speculation ranging to the uttermost bounds of thought, appealed to him. His most popular and most enduring work, *The Winning of the West*, although a history in form, in its inspiration was an assault upon what he regarded as the stupid and blameworthy indifference of the East to epochal events and heroic men beyond the Mississippi. His *Thomas H. Benton* owes most of its merit to Roosevelt's battering at the widespread impression that Old Bullion was no more than a pompous fraud, a wind-bag of colossal proportions. When there really was nothing to fight, as in his *Gouverneur Morris,* his book was no good.

Naturally, he reached the top of his form when he engaged in straight polemics, belaboring the Democrats or—usually with far more gusto—some deviant from the True Faith as Roosevelt perceived and proclaimed it, whether in politics, science, literature, strategics, geography, or the heresy of those who could not believe with him that birth control amounts to race suicide. Curiously enough, he never displayed racial or religious intolerance, probably because his early environment and training had instilled in him the conviction that fanaticism of that kind was ungentlemanly.

Like the bobtailed fox—and, if we are honest about it, like you and me—he erected his disability into a virtue. The strenuous life, being a psychological and perhaps a physical necessity to Roosevelt, became in his eyes the ideal life for all mankind. He preached it constantly and whenever he had the power he enforced it. As commander-in-chief of the army he compelled flabby and senescent generals to abandon their comfortable swivel chairs and take to the saddle. Naturally, the strain was too much for their cardiovascular systems, and the old boys died off in great numbers, which was perhaps a good thing for the army, but was not the effect intended. His close associates in the Cabinet and in other government offices he also put through rigorous physical disciplines, and few of them reached the age of seventy except such stiff-necked characters as Elihu Root, William H. Taft, Oscar Straus and James Wilson, who could not be bullied into hurling heavy medicine balls and careering through brush and brier on cross-country hikes.

The impression produced upon the country by all this was one of exuberant vitality, although the fact was that Roosevelt died worn out at sixty years and three months. Wilson, although broken under the burden of a great war, lasted to sixty-seven, and the second Roosevelt, battered by a depression and a double war, reached sixty-three. By comparison with these, Theodore Roosevelt's seven years in the White House were relatively easy, which arouses the suspicion that his strenuosity was less exuberant than frantic; he dared not proceed at a normal pace for fear of yielding to his early weakness and falling behind, and so he exhausted his strength prematurely.

However, the show he put on fitted exactly the mood of an exuberant nation and was the greatest success since Andrew Jackson put on a curiously similar show two generations earlier. His attack on the huge business combinations known as trusts roused tremendous enthusiasm. Students of economic history in the years since have raised serious doubt that his assault did any material damage to the trusts, but that he did serious psychological damage to the purse-pride of rich men is beyond question. They who had been obsequiously termed Captains of Industry were now scornfully branded as Malefactors of Great Wealth; and great was that fall.

The wrath of the deflated was correspondingly great, yet the truth is that Roosevelt, like his cousin a generation later, was making a necessary and inevitable readjustment, and making it probably at the smallest possible expense to the wealthy. The Gilded Age was over. The period of ruthless and arrogant exploitation both of natural resources and of labor had come to an end and the only question was whether wealth should dismount from its high horse feet first, or be thrown off and land on its head. Roosevelt compelled it to dismount and thereby saved it from being thrown; but his thanks consisted of bitter and reckless vituperation.

It may be argued with some plausibility that here is the point at which he joined the Lunatic Fringe because this was in fact the point of his highest sanity. He saw what was necessary and did it, in spite of the fact that a majority of the very people he was helping could not perceive the necessity. The man who not only sees what is the necessary next step but is willing to take it is almost always regarded as a lunatic by his contemporaries. If an easy and prosperous life is the *summum bonum,* then he is in fact a lunatic; for his attitude is an absolute guarantee of storm and stress, and more than a promise of loss and poverty.

To Theodore Roosevelt, however, ease and prosperity were not the *summum bonum;* his most industrious detractors must give him that. The swinish doctrine that man can live by bread alone he regarded with a loathing in which there was no trace of pretense; and it was this that lifted him to his high place.

To the fury and disgust of that prince of intellectuals, Henry Adams, Roosevelt posed as an intellectual. He was, of course, almost a textbook case of the emotional type, but he had not merely been exposed to education at Harvard, he had really taken it. His interests were wide-ranging and, if superficial, were acute. He invited to the White House such odd creatures as the mansion had not sheltered within living memory—philosophers, historians, novelists, poets, dramatists and sociologists. He brought in boxers, wrestlers and pole-vaulters, too, but they startled the politicians much less than did the scholars. Roosevelt did more than any President since the Virginia Dynasty to make it respectable to admit having read a book; so in his environment he was something of an intellectual and the waspish comments of Henry Adams do not alter the fact.

However, the most complete and flawless success of Theodore Roosevelt's career was not as *pater patriae* but as *pater familias.* He was a supremely great family man because he worked at it as hard as he worked at anything in his life. The wisdom and grace of his letters to his children raise them to a level not surpassed by any correspondence of that sort in the English language; but the final proof of his supremacy in this respect is not anything that he did, but in the record of his children. One died in battle for his country and another in its uniform; all have served it honorably, and none has brought reproach upon it.

No man ever brought up six fine citizens of the republic without diligence and labor, wisdom and patience. This facet of Roosevelt's character is so nearly perfect that it reduces criticism to impotence and silence. Yet there is all too much reason to fear that in this respect his aberration from the normal was greatest of all. In the modern world a man who works hard, constantly and brilliantly at the job of being a good father is, if not exactly a lunatic, certainly an odd character. Which is one of the things most conspicuously wrong with the modern world.

His misfortune was that, like most humorless men, as he grew older he carried the intensity of his convictions from principles over to methods. He believed in Americanism intensely, but in his fifties he began to confuse Americanism with the policies he had adopted in its support, and this led to a conviction that men who opposed him were opposing Americanism; so when one of those men proved consistently successful Roosevelt hated him as he hated Benedict Arnold, and for precisely the same reason.

His venomous detestation of Woodrow Wilson is often attributed to personal spleen at being superseded and there is little doubt that jealousy did play some part in it. Wilson was always the better scholar, which was bad enough, but in time he proved also to be the cleverer politician, which was intolerable. With his solemn devotion to clichés Roosevelt conceived of the academic life as cloistered and apart from reality, especially the realities of politics. He was incapable of realizing that while politics has as many variants as there are organizations among men, these variants differ mainly in the language and gestures conventionally employed. It never occurred to him that a man cannot be the successful president of a large university without being a masterly politician. Because the academician is suave and soft-spoken, it is rarely apparent to party leaders that when it comes to really dirty political fighting the average university faculty could give lessons to Tammany or any other party machine.

The truth was that Wilson had learned political strategy and tactics in a school tougher than any that Roosevelt had ever seen. Johns Hopkins, Bryn Mawr, Wesleyan and Princeton had taught him how to handle not merely Sugar Jim Smith, the kind of man that Roosevelt himself could handle, but also Clemenceau, the Tiger, and Lloyd George, the Eel, against whom Roosevelt would have had no more chance than a one-legged man has in a foot race.

This gross misconception of his opponent's ability was perhaps inevitably followed by an equally gross misconception of his motives. The qualification "perhaps" is necessary because not all Republican leaders were deceived. William H. Taft, for example, in some ways inferior to Roosevelt, was in this respect vastly his superior. Even Elihu Root, in spite of his conservatism and although in the end he allowed Roosevelt to drag him along, at first realized the logical necessity of Wilson's course at Paris and was inclined to give him support. But Roosevelt was implacable and he stiffened the resolution of his instrument, the elder Henry Cabot Lodge, to defeat Wilson at any cost, even at the cost of the ruin of the world.

Some allowance must be made for the fact that Roosevelt was a sick man and his physical condition no doubt impaired his judgment. But facts are facts. The interview between Lodge and Roosevelt, described by Roosevelt's sister and corroborated by Lodge, is in retrospect one of the most appalling incidents in American history. For then and there, before the peace conference had begun and while Wilson was on his way to Paris, these two concocted a scheme to defeat *any* treaty that Wilson might bring back. The idea was not to attack the treaty directly, but to offer a series of reservations, and if Wilson accepted the first series, to offer another, and more and more, until he would be compelled to take a stand. Then action would be delayed until the election of 1920, when the Republicans hoped to win the Presidency and would be in position to write a treaty of their own.

Political, social, moral irresponsibility could not go further. In that hospital room defeat of the League of Nations was assured; and with the League reduced to impotence, the way was cleared for Mussolini and then for Hitler. With the collective security represented by the League turned into a mockery, there was no agency by which Russia could be brought back into the family of nations until Communism had run its course. And all to prevent the Democratic party from controlling the country for another four years!

Here, then, was a leader whose career out of office took the opposite direction from his career in office. As President he perceived the necessity for wealth to assume an increasingly heavy burden of social responsibility. In his public pronunciamentos he urged it in moralistic style because that was the most effective style from the platform, but in private he added to the appeal to conscience an appeal to enlightened self-interest. He believed that wealth must assume social responsibility if for no higher reason than ordinary prudence. He was certain that irresponsibility, continued long enough, would bring fearful reprisals, if not destruction, upon capitalism. He was called a madman for harboring such opinions, but time has shown that his supposed madness was in reality an unusually clear perception of basic truth.

On the other hand, his career in opposition, after he left the White House, was in flat defiance of the trend of events. History took a turn that he did not expect when the First World War dealt a mortal wound not merely to the German empire, but to all imperialism. That he had not bargained for, and he refused to accept it; so he consistently misread the future, not only refusing to take the logical next step, but acting powerfully to prevent the country from taking it. For this he was hailed as a sound American, not misled by the iridescent dreams of the moonstruck.

Obviously, one direction must have been less rational than the other; and after forty years there is little doubt that it was when he was being described as a lunatic that Theodore Roosevelt was most completely sane, and when he swung the other way that posterity must dismiss him with a sigh as a once-good man who unfortunately developed hallucinations.

3

proem

Theodore Roosevelt, never a grave-robber and always a hearty fighter, usually reserved his objurgations for men who could and were expected to hit back. When he wrote in his autobiography of the Lunatic Fringe he was indeed referring to events then some years in the past; but when he used the words in his speeches the rejoicing galleries knew that he had in mind persons who were decidedly alive and kicking.

However, a single scornful reference leaves us in no doubt that he included in the group one man who had been dead for generations. This was Thomas Paine, the propagandist of the Revolution. In fairness to Roosevelt it should be pointed out that this reference, as false as it was venomous, was a casual aside, not a considered estimate, and was made when Roosevelt was a relatively young man and almost certainly unacquainted with Paine's writings, to say nothing of his life.

Nevertheless, the epithet throws a glaring light upon the opinion of Tom Paine current in educated circles in 1888. It tells us more about the America of the period than it does about Roosevelt; and the depth to which Paine's reputation descended gives the story its dramatic contrast.

Let us then turn back the clock from the Square Deal to the Revolution and its aftermath, strongly if rather luridly illumined in the tale of:

THOMAS PAINE

who was smitten by the people,
not the law

"THESE ARE THE times that try men's souls," wrote Tom
Paine in the opening paragraph of *The Crisis,* and in the
closing paragraph of the same essay he added, "I thank God
that I fear not."

With these two sentences the first great member of the
Lunatic Fringe qualified for inclusion in that body. He saw
that the souls of Americans were being tried as by fire, and
he had no fear of the outcome. Obviously he was a lunatic.

The story, perhaps apochryphal, is that he wrote in an
army field tent, using a drumhead for a writing desk; but
however that may be, there is no doubt whatever that he
wrote the opening paragraph and probably the closing one
in Washington's camp at a desperate moment in the history
of the Revolution. The fortunes of the American cause were
at their lowest ebb. Washington had fought on Long Island
and had been beaten. He had fought at White Plains and
had been beaten. He had been driven out of New York,
across New Jersey and into Pennsylvania. His army of 20,000
men had dwindled through casualties, prisoners, and, most
of all, desertion, to a few hundreds. To all human appear-
ances the war was lost.

Which was the moment that Tom Paine chose to announce,
"Thank God, I fear not."

It was insane. It was as wildly insane as the utterance of
those Americans who, ten years after the Second World War,

were asserting in the face of the Russian menace that all we had to fear was fear itself, an irrational fear that would betray us into surrendering liberty for a little temporary safety. Nevertheless, Washington was so enchanted that he issued orders that in every unit *The Crisis* should be read aloud to the troops at the very next formation, were it only a corporal's guard. More than that, the essay—doubtless expanded somewhat when Paine got back to Philadelphia—was printed and circulated throughout the country with immense effect.

As Crane Brinton points out, it is nonsense to suppose that *The Crisis* won the battle of Trenton; but it is equally nonsensical to doubt that it stimulated enormously the morale of a dispirited army, and three weeks later that army went out and won the battle. Circulated behind the lines it had an equal effect on the morale of a dispirited people, and every authority on the art of war, from Clausewitz down, agrees that the defeat of a nation consists in breaking its will to resist. Defeating its armies and occupying and devastating its territory are only means to that end. Victory comes when the will to resist is broken, and not before.

Paine's earlier essay, *Common Sense,* had done much toward establishing the will to resist, and this second one (the first of a series of twelve, usually grouped under the name of the first, *The Crisis*) without any doubt whatever helped to sustain that will. In short, there is no gainsaying that Paine was a tremendously important force on the psychological as distinguished from the military side of the Revolutionary War. He shared the military adventure. He was with the army through the dreadful retreat across New Jersey, although it is doubtful whether his status was that of a staff officer or that of a political agent. But the fact of his presence there, where he ran an excellent chance of being shot, or of being captured and hanged, establishes his physical courage; at the same time, it is beyond question that his military value was trifling by comparison with his value as a propagandist. Washington, seeing that, soon put him back beyond the reach of any roving enemy patrol; for as commander-in-chief he would sooner have lost a regiment of infantry than have had Tom Paine captured.

All this is merely by way of establishing the fact that Thomas Paine could say with Othello, "I have done the state some service, and they know 't." Congress knew it when a special act was passed conferring American citizenship on Paine, although he was born in England; and the people of New Jersey knew it when they gave him a farm near Bordentown. The great profits of his writings had gone to serve the cause, for, like most idealists, he was a hopelessly bad business man.

These honors came because by the course of events, not by any act of the man himself, the lunacy of 1776 had been converted into magnificent prophecy. After Washington won the war it became an article of faith that those who had been afraid were the lunatics while those who, like Paine, had no fear, were sane and rational. For several years following the Revolution—until 1789 to be exact—he held the status of a major prophet and all Americans were eager to do him honor.

Yet later he lost his standing so completely that after a hundred years Theodore Roosevelt, a product of Harvard and a writer of books—therefore presumably an educated man—could describe Paine as a "filthy little atheist." In life Paine stood five feet ten inches, was rather fastidious in his dress, and believed in God; what made him, after death, filthy, little, and an atheist was nothing of his own doing, but the fact that Roosevelt was writing the life of Gouverneur Morris and felt it necessary to defend that indefensible character. To do him justice it should be added that Roosevelt, in 1888, probably had not read *The Age of Reason,* but simply accepted the clerical opinion of the book; but his characterization of Paine was so widely accepted that it caused hardly a ripple of protest at the time.

The descent from prophet to pariah therefore illuminates not so much the character of Paine as that of the American people who demonstrated by their treatment of this man their vulnerability to a common human weakness that makes self-government an art painfully acquired and laboriously practiced. This weakness is inability to endure contradiction without flying into blind rage.

Tom Paine is dead. What he was capable of doing was done nearly two centuries ago and he has left the scene. Indeed, he has disappeared with singular completeness, for even his bones went into a junk shop and were lost there. His body, having been refused interment in consecrated ground, was buried in a field in New Jersey; but years later that strange creature William Cobbett exhumed the bones, intending to give them honorable burial in England; but Cobbett himself died before he could do so and his effects, including the bones, went to a dealer in second-hand furniture, which is the last we know of them.

But although Paine is dead, the American people survive and their attitudes and beliefs continue to have important effects upon the whole world. Logicians may contend that there is not, and cannot be, any such thing as the character and temperament of a nation, but only the sum of the characters and temperaments of the individuals composing the nation; but, unfortunately for the logicians, they are defeated by brutal facts. In every large population there is a dominant opinion, usually—it is a temptation to say invariably— the opinion of a minority.

If we are to believe John Adams, only one third of the Americans of 1776 really favored independence; another third went along pretty halfheartedly and the remaining third definitely favored monarchy. Even the genuine enthusiasts were a composite group; some of them, as for instance Thomas Jefferson, really hated oppression as such, while others, as for instance John Hancock, merely hated being oppressed. Their common detestation of British tyranny made them indistinguishable as long as the struggle against the King continued; but when that struggle was won their divergence promptly came to light. The particularist group regarded with suspicion any further interest in freedom as an abstraction; and if that interest seemed to involve danger their suspicion was converted into opposition that, in measure as the danger seemed to increase, mounted to hysteria.

That was the picture after 1783, and its resemblance to the picture in 1957 needs no emphasis. We still have people convinced that oppression of Americans is a special case not necessarily related to oppression of any other people; and we still have those who, like Paine, are persuaded that oppression is the disease and whether it breaks out in New Jersey or in Burma is of as little importance as whether a metastasizing cancer breaks out next in the foot or in the eye.

Neither of these constitutes a majority of the nation, but whichever happens to be dominant at the moment establishes for all practical purposes the opinion of the nation. As in John Adams' day at least one third of all Americans—pessimists will say more than one half—had no opinion of their own, so today there is a tremendous segment of the inert that will be carried along by whichever of the living opinions is most dynamic.

The historical record shows the fact—but does not explain it—that in the years following every great war the inert are swept along by the dominant opinion of the terrified. It is an odd characteristic of Americans that facing a clear and present danger, such as an attack by an armed enemy, they are as cool as the proverbial cucumber, but when the danger is merely potential, the dreadful thing that might happen "if," they go mad with fear and throw away their most cherished possessions in the hopeless attempt to attain certain security against contingent disaster.

In the decade following the Revolution we passed the Alien and Sedition laws. In that following the Civil War we abolished eleven states and converted them into military districts. In that following the First World War we staged the Mitchell Palmer witch-hunt. In that following the Second World War we set up the Attorney General's subversive list and the theory of guilt by association. In each of these cases the armed enemy had been defeated and the imminent danger averted before the extreme terror possessed us. In each case what we sought to guard against was not conquest, but conversion; so each represented a profound revolt against one of the basic theories of the republic, namely, "the safety with which error of opinion may be tolerated where reason is left free to combat it."

The story of the American people's dealings with Thomas Paine is one of the most deplorable revelations of a national weakness. It was in France that Paine was sent to jail for his opinions, not in this country. In this country he was merely sent to Coventry. But this means only that the case smirched the record of the people, not that of the government.

In the middle of the twentieth century, as at the beginning of the nineteenth, Americans will readily admit that it is a horrible heresy, political as well as religious, to assume that whatever is legal is *ipso facto* moral; but many respectable persons, or at least of enough respectability to be elected to Congress, are unable to perceive that the reverse of that medal is the assumption that a man who has not been punished by the criminal law has suffered no punishment at all. They hold that for the government to destroy a man's reputation, expose him to public contumely and contempt, and deprive him of the means of livelihood is not punishment; therefore the man involved is not entitled to the safeguards against unjust punishment allowed to persons accused of crime.

It was this sort of thing to which Tom Paine was subjected. It was precipitated by his adherence to the French Revolution after the well-to-do in America had begun to be frightened by the extent of the thing. In 1789 the Revolution was popular in this country because most people assumed that it was essentially a repetition of our own "revolution" which was, in fact, merely a civil war in which one segment of the British Empire revolted successfully against the political control of London. Neither John Adams nor Jefferson, to say nothing of Washington, dreamed of attempting to upset the whole social order.

So when Paine went to France with the avowed intention of encouraging the revolutionists his course was widely approved. Even when the enthusiastic French voted to give him French citizenship they were doing no more than the American Congress had done and his acceptance of the honor seemed to be in line with Lafayette's acceptance of American citizenship for himself and his descendants. It was not until it became apparent that the French revolutionists were attacking not only the institutions of monarchy and hereditary aristocracy, but also the institution of property and the lives of the propertied, that the opinion of the influential in this country began to shift. But then it shifted completely. American terror of the Jacobins mounted to heights not to be touched again until terror of the communists reached and surpassed that level a century later.

Paine, it is true, was not a Jacobin. In the National Assembly he had voted against the execution of the King and he joined the Gironde, a group of moderates roughly comparable to the Russian Mensheviki of 1917. But he had written one of his characteristic pamphlets in defense of the ideals of the Revolution, and this pamphlet, *The Rights of Man*, had what gentlemen of property considered a sinister success, both in this country and in England. In the latter country, by then at war with France, Paine was tried *in absentia* and outlawed; in the United States, not at war, he was merely ostracized by the upper classes. They lost control of the government in 1801, or they would probably have followed the British example when fear of the Jacobins was followed by fear of Napoleon.

However, Paine's moderation recoiled upon him when the Revolution began to devour its children. The Gironde then began to follow the aristocrats to the guillotine, and when the Terror reached its full height Paine found himself in prison. He appealed to the American minister, at that time Gouverneur Morris, an appointee of President Washington, and Morris, in Paine's opinion, betrayed him. Later Morris claimed that he refused to press Paine's case fearing merely to precipitate his execution, an explanation accepted by such conservative historians as Crane Brinton, but indignantly rejected by such radicals as Howard Fast. Certain it is that Morris informed the French government that Paine's claim to American citizenship had no foundation, in which Mr. Morris by his own fiat repealed an act of Congress.

If we may judge by his conduct in another case a little earlier the truth probably is that Mr. Morris had no particular desire to see Paine's head fall into a basket but, on the other hand, neither had he any objection to that outcome. The elegant Mr. Morris simply couldn't be bothered with the claims of down-at-the-heels patriots. His own diary records his intense annoyance at being called away from a party of ladies in 1792 to attest the will of a beggarly American who was dying in Paris. The attestation of an American officer was necessary to make the will valid, so Morris disgustedly went to the lodging house where the sick man was living; but as soon as he had signed the documents he hurried back to his ladies, leaving the American to fall across the bed and die untended and alone, his body face down on the bed, his feet touching the floor. The man was John Paul Jones, captain in the American Navy and sometime commander of the *Bonhomme Richard.*

A man capable of such treatment of our first great naval hero certainly could not be expected to do much for a minor hero of Tom Paine's class, but it is too much to assume that Morris deliberately tried to send him to the guillotine. Mr. Morris merely refused to concern himself with a character not accepted in the polite society that Mr. Morris adored. So Paine remained in prison until the worst of the terror was over and then James Monroe, successor to Morris, succeeded in getting him released.

Then Paine played the fool, utterly and ruinously. His contempt for Gouverneur Morris was so towering that it betrayed him into supposing Morris incapable of doing anything on his own initiative, which implied that he was acting on orders from the President. So Paine damned himself to lasting infamy by writing Washington a letter including the words, "I shall continue to think you treacherous until you give me cause to think otherwise." An American who would accuse Dwight D. Eisenhower of treachery would thereby ruin himself; imagine, then, the effect of such an accusation brought against George Washington!

But the letter was as manna from heaven to prosperous gentlemen who quaked in their boots with fear that the American masses might be stirred to rise against property rights. It gave them a terrible weapon, not only against Paine, but against all ideas harbored by Paine. Prosperous gentlemen were now joined by another class, only less influential in the United States, to wit, the clergy. During his enforced leisure in prison Paine had spent part of his time writing a document called *The Age of Reason.* It opens with the profession, "I believe in one God, and no more; and I hope for happiness beyond this life," and today it seems to be no more than an attack on what we now call fundamentalism. But the clergy chose to view it as an attack on all religion, thereby revealing the sacerdotal view that belief in God is immaterial, it is disbelief in the clergy that makes an atheist.

These were the factors that made Thomas Paine for a hundred years an untouchable in the country that he had served faithfully and brilliantly. He was not the victim of a tyrannous government. Indeed when the treaty of Amiens made it safe for Paine to return from France the then President, Jefferson, offered him passage on the *Maryland,* a naval vessel; but Paine, for once in his life exhibiting discretion, refused the offer and returned on an ordinary merchantman. He was the victim not of a tyrannous government, but of a tyrannous public opinion; which makes his story one to be pondered less by politicians than by the plain people of the United States; for the onus lies upon them.

Is it worth studying? That is to say, is there the faintest hope that any good purpose may be served by raking up

> Old, unhappy, far-off things,
> And battles long ago,

when the force involved is not the ruthlessness of some despot, but the attitude of the people? A tyrannical government can be overthrown, if needs must, by force and violence; but a tyrannical public opinion is invulnerable to physical weapons.

Philosophers from Plato down have despaired of an answer; or, perhaps, one should say that the *Phaedo* is their despairing answer. The Kremlin at this moment is grimly certain that the cup of hemlock is the people's invariable reward to Socrates; hence the Kremlin assumes that the people cannot be trusted with the advancement of civilization. We can retort, *"Tu quoque,"* but "You're another" has always been a puerile form of argument. It is true, but not much better, to argue that the ordeal of Oppenheimer, Edward U. Condon, Jessup and Lattimore is preferable to that of the old Bolsheviki. To prove our case we need to do more than prove that we do not physically exterminate brilliant servants of the state the moment they deviate from the party line; we need to prove that we do not even ostracize them for deviationism, and that is difficult.

Nevertheless, we are committed. The moment we proclaimed the pursuit of happiness as one of the inalienable rights of man we bound ourselves to accept the thesis that error of opinion may be tolerated where reason is left free to combat it. If that thesis is unsound, we are sunk, and the American Dream is no more than a dangerous hallucination.

But where is the indisputable evidence that it is unsound? It is beside the point to cite the New Deal because the New Deal is too recent for us to know what its ultimate fruits are destined to be. So far, indeed, the net result of the New Deal is only a series of reforms under which the country has attained an astounding power and prosperity; if it has, in fact, undermined the character of the people, that effect will not become plain for another generation, so it cannot be offered in evidence now.

If we go back far enough to be certain that we know the results, we find the lunacies of the Lunatic Fringe falling into two classes: those, such as the phalansteries of Fourier, that inflicted only microscopic damage on the country and have long been forgotten, and those, such as most of the speculations of Thomas Paine, that have turned out to be not lunacy at all, but prophecy.

The long-lasting and incalculable damage that the country has suffered from ideas have almost invariably come from some idea that the Lunatic Fringe denounced but that was approved by the wise and prudent. The Alien and Sedition laws were not put through by the wild radicals, but by conservatives. This has been true of every effort to repress opinion, down to the Espionage Act of Wilson's administration and the test oaths of the Truman-Eisenhower regime.

Safety, therefore, seems to lie in the direction of persuading the wise and prudent, rather than the lunatics, that the framers of the Constitution knew what they were about when they defined treason as consisting only of overt acts proved by the testimony of two or more witnesses. That rules out legal punishment for moral treason; but we seek avidly to punish it by extra-legal means, and the Supreme Court has found that in recent years we have adopted illegal means in more than one case.

We are reluctant to face the fact that the suppression of unpopular opinions is itself moral treason in that it tends to subvert the Constitution. This reluctance is natural, but it is one of those natural bents, like the natural impulse to brain an enemy, that must be eradicated if civilization is to advance. To tolerate "opinions that we loathe and believe fraught with death," as Justice Holmes described them, is tremendously difficult, but it is one of the qualifications of a civilized man.

And it is the task of the individual. People like Tom Paine are hard to bear, and no institution can make it easier for us to stand them. But it must be done, for some among them are not the lunatics that all appear to be, but Promethean messengers who have stolen Vulcan's fire for the use of mankind. So the individual American who uses, or approves the use of legal or extra-legal means to suppress opinion is recreant to the duty that lies upon us all, even though we have not taken the President's oath, to "preserve, protect and defend the Constitution of the United States."

4

proem

The explosion—it is the only adequate word—of intellectual energy that occurred on this continent in the last third of the eighteenth century and that continued to flash and sparkle di-minuendo through the first quarter of the nineteenth was a phe-nomenon that much study has done little to explain.

Why a single country, and that one a remote backwater of civilization rather less important than Turkey is today, should have been endowed all at once—that is to say, within what the Psalmist declared is the normal span of life—with such thinkers as Wythe, Mason, Taylor of Caroline, the Adams cousins, Frank-lin, Dickinson, Jefferson, Hamilton, Madison and Jay, with the young Marshall rapidly developing, is a dark mystery. It is the more impenetrable when one reflects that these were supported by a phalanx of orators and organizers of the calibre of Henry, Morris, the Lees and the Pinckneys, with the unique figure of Washington brooding over all.

It couldn't last. By 1830 the grand fireworks display was over. Political genius flashed occasionally in Webster and Clay, and smouldered in Calhoun, but philosophy, as Jefferson and John Adams understood it, took a long vacation as far as the United States was concerned. The pendulum swung from Enlighten-ment to Obscurantism and minds grew dull. But not life. These years may have been short on intellectuality, as compared with the Revolutionary period, but they had their uproars, less edifying, no doubt, but decidedly more amusing than the Discourses on Davila *or the* Letters of a Pennsylvania Farmer, *and not without significance for the future of the republic.*

By way of illustration, let us attend to the tale of:

SARAH AND ANGELINA GRIMKÉ

who were themselves to admiration

TO RE-CREATE the intellectual atmosphere of an earlier century is patently impossible, and to establish anything like an adequate understanding of it is difficult in the extreme; but it is just such considerations that make the laborer in the historical vineyard worthy of his hire. When, however, the difficulties presented by mere chronology are multiplied by others arising from psychological idiosyncrasies, the difficulty proceeds to the verge and perhaps beyond the verge of the impossible. For this reason no candid writer will present his work on such a subject without prefacing it with a sharp *caveat* to the reader, lest he accept as oracular what is in reality nine-tenths speculative. When you read interpretations of the oddities of the past, read with your fingers crossed.

The story of the Grimké sisters is a case in point. A twentieth-century inquirer, carefully examining the records and discarding all those whose authenticity is questionable, might well enough be led to the conclusion that is is flatly impossible that these women should have existed. Oh, it is easy to concede that certain individuals bearing the name may have subsisted at a certain time, and may have spoken and acted as is recorded. But the Grimkés, we are told, were not merely individuals, they were important persons, exerting a very considerable influence on public affairs; and that is all but incredible.

It is incredible, that is to say, if you share this writer's conviction that in a democracy it is rare, perhaps unheard of, for anyone to attain a position of influence without possessing some qualities that commend themselves to a reasonable mind. Under a rigid social order it may be otherwise. If your father is a king you are influential throughout the realm, irrespective of your personal character and intelligence; but in a society organized without reference to heredity, the individuals who rise to the top have some sort of buoyance of their own.

Importance is not identical with influence. Notoriety has a certain importance. If you have burned the temple at Ephesus, or shot President Garfield, you are assured of a place in history, but the influence you wield is minus, strictly a negative quantity. Swindlers may exercise great influence, as Cagliostro and Rasputin did, but a really great swindler has some kind of personal magnetism, beyond analysis yet incontestably real; that sort of thing, however, vanishes with its possessor and escapes the historian. Yet propagandists while they may be swindlers and are nearly always exhibitionists, do not as a rule achieve large success unless there is in them some residuum with a value whose solidity may be detected even in the dark backward and abysm of time.

The Grimké sisters achieved what was, at the time and in their situation, large success. It follows that there must have been merit in them, presumably something more than their obvious courage and intellectual vigor. To the inquiring reporter writing these pages their merit seems to be plain; but it must be admitted that the next student may not be able to see it at all, or be unwilling to grant that it was merit. It is elusive and their demerits are not. The Grimkés were colossal nuisances, literally continental nuisances, and the evil they did is as conspicuous in American history as is the Monument in the topography of Washington; but their sound and admirable contribution is largely speculative and should be so presented. In the following pages is a suggestion of what—other than fairly ribald entertainment—the Grimkés were good for; but it is only a guess which the reader should accept just to the extent that it checks with his own experience.

Sarah Moore Grimké and her sister, Angelina Emily, who married Theodore Weld, were South Carolina aristocrats who, between 1830 and 1835, turned Abolitionist and later Feminist and raised hell (for Sherman said war is hell) all over the country for thirty years.

That is the story in its simplest terms, but attempts to define those terms have already run into many volumes, probably with many more to come.

For example, the term "South Carolina aristocrat" is hardly less vague than the term "Boston Brahmin" that all philosophy has not yet been able to define exactly. Both are as extinct as the dodo, and in each case the term is now applied to a creature different from and in many respects diametrically opposite to the sort of thing it meant a century and a quarter ago. Furthermore, these palmetto aristocrats were peculiar even in a class all of whose members were peculiar by modern standards. Finally, they flourished in a period when the prevailing mode of thought in America was fast, furious and astonishing; and their mode of thought was faster, more furious, and more astonishing than the average.

On the paternal side their inheritance was a cross between French and German, on the maternal side straight English Puritan. The patronymic Grimké is German, but their father's middle name was Faucheraud, derived from his mother's family, Huguenots who settled in Charleston after the

revocation of the Edict of Nantes. Huguenot blood is itself
a cachet of distinction in Charleston and in the veins of a
family that has gained eminence by its own efforts it is a double distinction.

Then this John Faucheraud Grimké, not only an aristocrat but an intellectual, educated at Cambridge and the
Middle Temple in London, married Mary Smith, great-
granddaughter of the second Landgrave of South Carolina.
A Landgrave was one of the weird inventions of John Locke
when he drew up the *Fundamental Constitutions* of the Caro-
linas and attempted to impose a landed aristocracy on the
colonies. This nobility included, in descending order, Lords
Proprietors, Landgraves, Caciques, Lords of Manors, and
Freeholders. It lasted only briefly, of course, but it is evident
that a man who was created a Landgrave and held 48,000
acres was a person of importance. Mary was if anything even
more of an aristocrat than her husband.

But they were South Carolina aristocrats, which is to say
they were differentiated sharply from both the English and
the Boston variety. Psychologically, they were closer to the
ancien régime in France—violent, brave, proud, and utterly
humorless, which last quality made them instinctive foes of
intelligence. They had their mutations and sports, of course,
but when a South Carolina aristocrat developed a really
strong and lively intelligence he usually suffered a degree of
ostracism; witness, for example, James L. Petigru who, when
a stranger asked to be directed to the insane asylum, had wit
enough to point the man to the hall where the Secession
Convention was sitting, and Joel Poinsett, scholar, statesman,
diplomatist and Secretary of War, whose singular fate it was
to have his name preserved in *poinsettia,* a flower that he
brought to this country from Mexico. Petigru and Poinsett
were both Andrew Jackson men during the Nullification
crisis, which means that they were at odds with their neigh-

bors; but wit and learning would have set them apart regardless of politics.

To some extent John Faucheraud Grimké in his earlier day was in the same class. For one thing, he took his education seriously. He became a good classical scholar at Cambridge and an even better lawyer at the Middle Temple. Returning to this country, he made a distinguished career at the bar and eventually on the bench, where he rose to be Senior Associate, virtually Chief Justice of South Carolina. There is no question of his learning in the law, but the rigidity of the Huguenot in his blood, reinforced by the rigidity of the Puritan in his wife, made him what is commonly known as "a hanging judge." The severity of his sentences was proverbial but it could not be denied that they were strictly according to law.

The evidence indicates that he was a bit of a hanging judge in the home, too, but his daughters, Sarah and Angelina, seem never to have developed much bitterness toward him on that account. Mary was the one who caught it. Formally, the Grimkés were Episcopalians, a sect by no means notorious for the austerity of its religious practices, but the Grimkés were exceptions. Massachusetts Bay itself could hardly produce a household in which the unfortunate children were held to a more rigorous code, and in later years they attributed it to their mother. No doubt there was some justice in this, but it should not be forgotten that Mary Grimké bore fourteen children, so sheer statistics prove that her maternal sympathy and understanding must have been spread pretty thin. She is entitled to the benefit of the doubt and there is certainly a reasonable doubt that the sternness for which she was remembered was her nature rather than a necessity imposed upon her by her situation.

As is usually the case, with some of the children it "took" and in others it produced rebellion. One son, Thomas, serious-minded from his youth up, was with difficulty dissuaded from entering the ministry; he studied law instead, and practiced successfully, but his main interest was in reform movements, mainly educational. In politics he was non-conformist enough to stand with Petigru and Poinsett against Nullification, but in education he was a strong believer in the Bible as the basis of intellectual training from the primary class to the university. However, he had some interesting ideas about vocational education and was beginning to attract national attention when he died at the age of forty-eight.

His brother Henry did not, to put it mildly, display any comparable hunger and thirst after righteousness. Henry is the Grimké whom all the eulogists of the family and, for that matter, the chroniclers of polite society studiously ignore. Henry is the skeleton in the Grimké closet, yet when one examines the record attentively there is nothing very lurid in it. Nobody suspected Henry of celebrating the Black Mass, or of engaging in bacchanalian orgies or any of the other appalling practices of the Hell-Fire Club.

One suspects, indeed, that the gravamen of his offending was his yielding to a comparatively decent impulse. His departure from the strait and narrow way occurred when, dissatisfied with his legal spouse, he took a Negro mistress and set up a second establishment. Charleston society regarded that as an offense, but certainly it was not an outrage thitherto unheard of; it had happened before without arousing more than a mild disapprobation. Where Henry Grimké passed beyond the pale was in blandly acknowledging the children the woman bore him and in doing what he could to protect them from the worst horrors of slavery. There was actually not a great deal that he could do. He has been accused of cynicism because in his will—he died in 1850—he provided that his Negro children were to go to their white half-brother, with a provision that they were not to be sold.

It is hard to detect cynicism in this, for at the time of his death outright manumission was illegal in South Carolina and the children, still quite young, could not be sent north without some sort of guardianship. What more could he do?

But sardonic fate made Henry Grimké's domestic arrangements glaringly conspicuous by endowing two of the boys with unusual intellectual ability. Archibald Henry Grimké grew up to become a lawyer, vice president of the National Association for the Advancement of Colored People, United States consul to Santo Domingo, and biographer of Garrison and Sumner. His brother Francis went into the ministry and served for fifty years as minister of the Fifteenth Street Presbyterian Church in Washington. Their exploits kept the name of Grimké familiar to the public for more than half a century after the white Grimkés had all died or sunk into obscurity.

The effect of a rigorous upbringing on the two girls followed a somewhat different pattern. In youth they were both pretty, according to contemporary accounts which, it must be admitted, are hard to believe if one has seen only their photographs in later years, for in those they are a pair of battle-axes. In any event, they were not originally of such formidable appearance as to be doomed from birth to be wallflowers and it is a reasonable assumption that they were fairly popular. Certainly their social position was such as to give them entrée everywhere.

The elder girl, Sarah Moore, even in her Charleston days was erratic enough to attract attention and to be remembered in later years. In one season she would be the gayest of the gay, a constant attendant at every ball, every excursion, every theater-party given in Charleston and a sparkling center of attraction at each; but the next season she would appear nowhere, living a life as secluded as that of a cloistered nun.

Obviously, the austerity of her upbringing was battling against a powerful impulse toward self-expression and the poor girl was torn between them.

The younger (by thirteen years), Angelina Emily, throughout her Charleston life was the demure type, too shyly quiet to be a resounding social success, but commanding the high approbation of all the local duennas as a very model of the perfect lady. Charleston was correspondingly astounded when it proved to be Angelina who imitated the monk of Siberia. In 1835 she burst from her cell with what Charleston could only regard as a hell of a yell in William Lloyd Garrison's Abolitionist magazine, the *Liberator,* and, after an amazing and increasingly clamorous career in the press and on the lecture platform, climaxed it by marrying what was, in South Carolina opinion, a fair approximation of the Devil.

Yet to lay all this to the credit, or charge, of Mary Smith and John Faucheraud Grimké would be distinctly unfair. The sisters cherished no great affection for their parents, especially their mother, and probably harbored a resentment against them that they did not fully recognize themselves. But the spirit of the times had a great deal to do with it—not merely the spirit of Charleston, but that of the whole country as well. No intellectual atmosphere could have been better designed to develop just such psychological quirks as they possessed, or were possessed by.

It was a time of tremendous economic and political ferment. The sheer speed of the country's expansion was throwing everything a little off balance, and mind and character were affected as well as markets and frontiers. The strain of Protestantism that originated at Geneva, was refined in Scotland, and refined again in Ulster, was dominant in religious affairs. Even those sects that never formally acknowledged the leadership of John Calvin were affected—the Methodists and Baptists being largely taken over, while the Lutherans and Episcopalians betrayed definite signs of Calvinism, and even the American Catholics showed some leaning if not toward Calvin at least toward Cornelis Jansen. The Genevan doctrine of salvation by bludgeon was perhaps more widely accepted in religious circles than ever before or since.

This movement was marked by two characteristics in direct conflict with the original doctrine of American liberty—in public relations a theocratic, in private an ascetic ideal. As she reached maturity Sarah Grimké accepted both. The precipitating influence seems to have been her removal from Charleston. At sixty-five the Judge's physical frame began to give way and eventually his doctors advised him to consult the celebrated Philip Syng Physick, of Philadelphia, called the "Father of American Surgery." As Dr. Physick was famous for his operation for renal calculi, that may have been Grimké's trouble; at any rate, it was plainly too serious for him to be permitted to go alone, so his daughter Sarah accompanied him. But after they had stayed some months in Philadelphia the doctor could do no more than recommend sea air, so Grimké removed to Long Branch, New Jersey, where he died in 1819, when Sarah was twenty-seven.

But in Philadelphia they had lived in the house of a Quaker family whose kindliness and sincerity made a great impression on Sarah. After burying her father at Long Branch she returned to Charleston by sea; on the boat were several Quakers with whom she spent much time during the voyage and with whom she maintained contact after her arrival. Like most intelligent Southerners from Washington and Jefferson down, the Grimkés had always deplored the slave system and the Quakers' strong opposition to that system, far from repelling her, was one of their chief merits in her eyes.

The eventual outcome was that she went to Philadelphia and became a Quaker, although not for some years. They

were bitter years, too, for Sarah was a strong-minded individual who associated, in fact identified with her religion an
almost pathological desire to dominate. Her final departure
was certainly a great relief to her and probably to a more or
less conventional family as well. A few years later she persuaded Angelina to join her, both in Philadelphia and in the
Quaker connection; it was, in fact, not difficult, for Angelina's shy exterior masked a drive toward self-expression exceeding Sarah's own.

They regarded themselves, of course, as humble instruments in the hands of the Lord and they delighted in mortification of the flesh; but there was about as much genuine
humility in them as there was in Benito Mussolini a hundred
years later. The evidence is the fact that when they joined
the Quakers, who practiced true humility, they found the
association intolerable. It never occurred to them that the
fault might be in themselves; they attributed it to hypocrisy
in the Quakers who, although they professed opposition to
slavery, were unwilling to resort to violence, even violence
in words, to advance the cause of Negro freedom. The
Grimkés remained in the Society of Friends for a few years
only.

But to assume that they were themselves hypocrites would
be to misunderstand the situation completely. On the contrary, they were utterly, terribly sincere. In an age not so
much materialistic in the usual sense, as wholly innocent of
any psychological subtlety, they never gave a thought to se-
curing wealth and ease, or even ordinary comfort for themselves; therefore they assumed that they were wholly altruistic, and the age agreed with them.* The idea that to

---

* Nor solely their own generation. As late as 1885 Catherine H.
Birney, daughter-in-law of James G. Birney, the Abolitionist opponent
of Garrison, wrote a dual biography of the Grimké sister which, in spite
of some inaccuracies, remains the best factual source; but its swooning
style whenever it touches their spiritual endowment tempts the modern reader to treat it somewhat jocosely.

deprive another of his moral and intellectual freedom of action is a worse offense than to rob him of his purse was alien to the time. Indeed, in the circles in which the Grimkés moved it was accepted as a high Christian duty to deprive a man of his liberty provided it were done for his own good.

In early Massachusetts this spirit was more conspicuous because there it had the full force of law behind it, but Puritanism in the worst sense of the word was no more arrogant and unreasoning in 1638 than it was in the half-century from 1825 to 1875. The exile of Anne Hutchinson, for example, had a great deal more common sense behind it (for Anne really was subversive) than Sarah Grimké had in 1828 when she persuaded Angelina to destroy her set of Scott's novels as a sacrifice to religion.

At that, the Grimkés were rather reasonable compared with some of the other busybodies, organized and unorganized, that flourished at the time. The Female Retrenchment Societies, for instance, mobilized to put pressure on women to eschew "tea, coffee, rich cake, pastry, preserves, snuff and tobacco, as well as wine and cordials." * There were the Tappan brothers (originally Toppan and English; not to be confused with descendants of Jurian Teunnisse Tappaan, the Dutch outfit whose name is preserved by the Tappan Sea), New York silk merchants, immensely rich, immensely pious, and immensely bigoted. The Tappans knew that they had to be right because they had begun poor and had become wealthy which, as everyone knew, meant that they had been favored by the Lord for their righteousness.

Before Angelina and her spouse came along, Arthur, the elder Tappan, was interested mainly in education and prostitution; he helped found Kenyon and Oberlin colleges and the Magdalen Society. Lewis, younger by two years, went in

* Thomas, Benjamin, *Theodore Weld*, p. 28. Thomas, whose genuine admiration of Weld stops short of adulation, compiles a fascinating if appalling list of such self-righteous meddlers.

for homiletics and missions; he seems to have started the fashion of renting or building a church and installing a popular preacher in it regardless of his creed. He was also a heavy supporter of the American Foreign Mission Society and the American Bible Society. It was the policy of the Tappan firm to fire any employee who entered a theater, played cards, smoked tobacco, or was seen speaking to an actress.

The Tappans were theoretical Abolitionists, of course, although as big business men they couldn't go along with Garrison when he called the Constitution "a compact with hell" and publicly burned a copy. Their interest in the cause was, in the early years, genuine, but not very active.

This is fairly dreadful, but let us complete the picture. These men were certainly not avaricious; it is clear that Lewis, for instance, never profited by a dollar from his churches although his imitators later turned the scheme into a very good thing indeed, financially. The brothers were generous with their time, as well as their money, and worked hard in support of many worthy projects. No doubt they did some good; but if so they had their reward in public adulation throughout their lives. There is no reason for a later generation to ignore the fact that their complacent moral certainty made them a pair of arrogant old dictators whose philosophy would have been as abhorrent to Thomas Jefferson as that of the Emperor Nero.

The suddenness with which the intellectual climate of America changed from the Enlightenment to this Outer Darkness is curiously illustrated by a third Tappan brother. Arthur was born in 1786, Lewis in 1788, which means that both came to years of awareness after the close of the Revolutionary period. But they had an older brother, Benjamin, born in 1773, therefore of voting age when John Adams was elected President. That is to say, he grew up while Adams, Jefferson and Hamilton were still dominant figures, and their political ideas permeated the mental atmosphere. As a United States Senator from Ohio, Benjamin Tappan was an anti-slavery man, but not an Abolitionist; and in his latter days he was known as "the hoary-headed skeptic" because of his frank dislike of emotional religion. In short, he was the antithesis of his younger brothers, the product of an earlier age.

So if the Grimké sisters thought to acquire merit by cutting to pieces the novels of Scott and depriving the working man of the solaces of beer and tobacco, they were in perfect tune with the spirit of the time, and to accuse them of hypocrisy would be fatuous. More than that, if they were congenitally aggressive in the early days they confined their aggression strictly to their own circle, largely to their relatives and close friends. It is certain that they said, and there is no reason to doubt that they believed, that they were propelled into public life against all their own inclinations.

It began with a letter that Angelina wrote in 1835 to William Lloyd Garrison, then just well launched on his incendiary career. Angelina did not intend it for publication, and she was aghast when it appeared in the pages of the *Liberator;* but once it was out, she stoutly refused to recant. The letter was a paean of praise to Garrison, not only for his work but for the way in which he was doing it, and it fell upon Charleston ears like a demonic screech. Angelina, demure little Angelina, was not only off the reservation, but war-painted and war-whooping in a way beyond belief!

This, remember, was only four years after Nat Turner's rebellion in which fifty-five white men, women and children were butchered, spreading horror and terror through all slave territory. In characteristic American fashion—still characteristic a hundred and twenty years later when the collapse of the Chinese Chiang Kai-Shek was charged to a mild-mannered college professor not even connected with the government—Southerners attributed the trouble to the malice of some personal devil and the obvious candidate was Garrison. The fact that illiterate slaves could not possibly have read the *Liberator,* or understood it if it had been read to them, was ignored; *anathema maranatha* was pronounced against Garrison and all connected with him. And it was this character that Angelina Grimké had publicly lauded!

Ostracism was instant and Sarah at first was appalled; but now Angelina emerged as the stronger character. After all, she wasn't the baby sister any longer; she was now thirty years old, and in the depths of those innocent blue eyes there lurked a fire not a whit less ardent than Garrison's incandescence. Angelina had not deliberately sought a fight, but since Charleston had asked for it, Charleston would get it.

Instead of a recantation, she turned out a thirty-six-page pamphlet entitled "Appeal to the Christian Women of the South," which instantly made her one of the leading Abolitionist propagandists and one of the most cordially hated. "The women of the South can overthrow this horrible system of oppression and cruelty, licentiousness and wrong," she wrote, and it blistered not only because there was some truth in it, but because it was deliberately contrived to incite a feminine revolt under the magnolias. The indignation of Samson complaining, "If ye had not plowed with my heifer . . ." was shared by the slaveholders against this person who was tampering with their womenfolk; and the fact that she was herself a Southern woman made it all the worse.

But the fat was in the fire now. "Oppression and cruelty, licentiousness and wrong," were characterizations of the Peculiar Institution too true to be forgiven by the South; and the sort of bird that befouls its own nest was a characterization too true to be forgiven by Angelina. So it was war to the knife thenceforth.

Anyhow, what Henry Watterson later called "the star-eyed goddess of Reform" was in the ascendant all over the country. It mattered little what one was reforming, as long as one was for Reform of some kind. Frequently it was the habits of the working class, as with the New York Association of Gentlemen, but it might be diet, as with the famous Dr. Sylvester Graham, or dress, as with Mrs. Amelia Bloomer. The all-important thing was to be for Reform; preferably, of course, the reform of someone else since, as Montaigne observed, "every man poiseth upon his fellowes sinne, and elevates his owne."

The Grimkés displayed an extremely catholic taste in the matter. They were ardent reformers of the working classes, of fallen women, of tobacco smokers and, of course, of drunkards. But they also adopted Dr. Graham's dietary fads and, for a time, Mrs. Bloomer's baggy trousers. As the years passed, however, all other reforms were pretty much absorbed and lost in the one great reform, the abolition of Negro slavery. This had the triple advantage of being obviously right, highly spectacular, and confined largely to the Southern states. It offered to the North the promises at once of economic profit by eliminating the competition of cheap labor, of moral sanctification, and, by lurid exaggerations of miscegenation, of erotic titillation.

But to certain individuals it offered another and even greater satisfaction, as modern historians have begun to perceive.* These were the psychologically Displaced Persons, particularly scions of old American stock in the Northeast. They were finding themselves pushed out by Irish and German immigrants, with already some infiltration from southern Europe, especially Portugal. Naturally they felt that the world was all wrong and wanted to fight somebody. It was not so much that the old Americans were being driven from

---

* For example, David Donald in *Lincoln Reconsidered* (1956) and before him Avery Craven and others.

their homes as that they were being deprived of the moral
and social superiority that they had so long enjoyed—a more
serious deprivation than physical displacement. The time
had not yet come when in Massachusetts the name of Ken-
nedy would be more potent than that of Lodge, but it was
plainly on the way, and the frustration of the sufferers needed
some vent. Abolition offered it.

Historian Donald has assembled statistical evidence that
of the really prominent Abolitionists eighty-five percent
were from the Northeast, sixty-five percent from New England, and thirty percent from Massachusetts alone. Into this
group of the displaced the Grimké sisters, although they
came from South Carolina, fit neatly enough. It was not indeed immigration that had displaced them, but a tempera-
mental inability to adjust to the intellectual atmosphere of
Charleston; but they belonged in the category of Displaced
Persons, all right.

This probably explains why they responded more ardently
to Garrison than to such a leader as James G. Birney, who
was an Abolitionist, but who cherished a constitutional objection to manslaughter as a method of reform. As a matter
of fact, even Garrison recoiled from the idea of effecting
abolition by gorging the vultures with human flesh and in
1861 favored letting the slave states go, dismissing preserva-
tion of the Union as a secondary matter. It was no man but
a woman who wrote the blood-dripping "Battle Hymn of
the Republic," a song so revoltingly ferocious that it makes
even "Maryland, My Maryland"—man-produced—seem pale
and ineffectual by comparison.

Then there was Theodore Dwight Weld. This apparition,
called by Donald "greatest of the Western Abolitionists," and
by Gilbert H. Barnes * flatly "greatest of the Abolitionists"

* In his sketch of Weld in the *Dictionary of American Biography*,
XIX, 627.

was born in Connecticut of very decidedly old American stock, having Edwards, Dwight and Hutchinson blood, and coming of a long line of Congregational ministers.

But he was an odd fish, physically and mentally. Described by his biographer, Thomas, as dark, with a twisted nose, a disfigured eye, and an "expression of severity," he is said by others to have had the look of "a pirate or a chief-inquisitor." Certainly no male observer would suppose this to be the answer to a maiden's prayer, yet Angelina Grimké's word for him from their first encounter was "archangel."

A psychiatrist might find significance in a curious mental quirk that harassed Weld from his youth up. It was a failure of memory so marked that not only could he never be sure of the day of the week or month but sometimes had to look out of the window to determine whether it was winter or summer, and would frequently lose a quarter of an hour looking for the spectacles that he held in his hand. So, naturally, he set up as an expert in memory training and in his early days had some success as a lecturer in mnemonics.

It is easy to believe that Theodore Weld, at odds with the world, simply had to fight somebody and sincerely preferred Goliath of Gath to any less formidable opponent. His first antagonist, however, was the Demon Rum, which he took on in a big way while still a ministerial student at Oneida Institute (this was long before John Humphrey Noyes set up the Oneida Community, of blushful memory, on the other side of the county). So prodigiously successful was Weld as a temperance lecturer that the Tappans vainly tried to enlist him to head up various reform projects in which they were interested. In the end it was Weld who, having transferred his interest to Abolition, enlisted the Tappans for his project. Up to this point their interest in Abolition, while sincere enough, had been rather languid, but Weld transformed them into flaming evangels, who thenceforth supplied him with the financial sinews of war.

Here at last he had the kind of Reform perfectly suited to his genius. Not only was it vast and formidable, but it had for the pathologically forgetful memory-training expert, the additional advantage that he didn't know a thing about it, having never, at this time, set foot below the Potomac. The slave system was eventually to be destroyed by men who knew a great deal about it—men such as Helper, who dynamited its social and economic theory, and others such as Birney, Benton of Missouri, Lincoln and, to do him justice, even wobbly old Martin Van Buren, all of whom joined in undermining its political theory.

Helper's statistics wrote doom upon the lowering front of the slave system as relentlessly as the ghostly finger wrote it upon Belshazzer's wall. The political philosophers turned its intellectual pretensions to ridicule. The thing was bound to collapse and it is often assumed that if it had fallen under its own weight slavery would have disappeared without civil war. No doubt it would; but there is always the chilling possibility that the South would have disappeared too, at least for many generations. The system was leading to utter economic and social collapse, and if that had occurred it would have meant the final evacuation of the white population and a hundred years of slow disintegration, after the fashion of San Domingo following the slave revolt.

So it is conceivable that the Abolitionists may have contributed in the end to the salvation of the region. Undoubtedly their energy, courage and hate, by arousing equal and opposite forces among the idiotic element in the South made war inevitable. But war had at least the effect of saddling the race problem on the whole Federal Union, instead of leaving the South to deal with it alone, and hopelessly. True, from 1876 to the First World War the rest of the country largely ignored its responsibility to the infinite damage of the South; but after 1917, when thirty-two percent of the Negro population moved into the North and West the obligation had to be faced, and hope of a civilized solution began to revive.

Be that as it may, for some fifteen years Theodore, Angelina and Sarah contributed heavily to the growing crisis. The alliance started when Theodore evolved an idea that was a stroke of genius. Having in mind perhaps Luke 10:1, he called together seventy disciples and, after a period of instruction, sent them out through the West to preach fiery Abolitionism. One of the seventy was blue-eyed Angelina, the windows of whose soul by this time must have had the tint, not of summer skies, but of a Bunsen burner. Their first encounter was singular, for Weld gave her a verbal flaying for what he considered some frivolity in her dress or demeanor and she fell in love with him on the spot. He was equally attracted, but it was two years before he dared propose and then it was done accidently, in a fit of remorse for having reduced her to tears by one of his apocalyptic thunderings.

Nevertheless, the marriage was a success, albeit of a strange kind. Shortly after the ceremony, performed in 1838, both partners were incapacitated for the lecture platform, Weld because he seems to have ruptured his vocal cords in thundering at the Seventy, Angelina by being thrown from a horse. However, the pen was left, and in 1839 Weld published his most famous bit of writing; since he had no personal acquaintance whatever with it, he wrote "American Slavery As It Is," the pamphlet that Harriet Beecher Stowe later said she "crystallized" into *Uncle Tom's Cabin*. Sarah, escaping physical disability, continued on the lecture platform, swinging more and more to Women's Rights, while Weld and Angelina contributed to the anti-slavery movement as pamphleteers and lobbyists up to the Civil War.

But even before the war the main interest of all three had been shifting to a school they conducted, first at Belleville, New Jersey, and later at Hyde Park, Massachusetts. Their methods were regarded as bizarre at the time, but some of them proved sound and have had an effect on the development of modern education; that record, however, belongs in the history of pedagogy rather than in that of the nation.

The war had been over for more than two years when Sarah chanced upon a newspaper item about a student who was making a brilliant record at Lincoln University, a Negro school in Pennsylvania, and who bore the name of Archibald Henry Grimké. With foreboding, Sarah wrote to the young man, hoping that he was merely a former slave who had taken the family name, but he replied to the sisters that he was indeed the son of Henry Grimké and their nephew.

Angelina fainted.

But they were Grimkés, who never recanted. Nothing could compel them to repudiate all they had been preaching for twenty years. They acknowledged their relationship to the boy and to his brother, Francis, perhaps with an unacknowledged determination not to be outdone in human decency by their reprobate brother. When Archibald finished at Lincoln the sisters gave him financial help to get through the Harvard Law School, and they assisted Francis in his theological studies at Princeton. Their efforts were justified, for both boys made good.

Sarah died at Hyde Park in 1873, aged eighty-one. Angelina died in 1879 at seventy-four. Theodore Weld reached the ripe old age of ninety-one, dying in 1895.

This is without doubt one of the most curious tales in the weird annals of the Lunatic Fringe, and an attempt to relate it to anything rational is a hazardous undertaking. The frenetic vituperation that Charleston poured upon the sisters was too obviously absurd to deserve comment. It defeated itself. But the adulation that tried—and for a long time with success—to elevate the Grimkés to the level of the saints and sages was equally ludicrous. It was engendered by the sentimentality that has made Americans easy victims of pharisaism in many forms.

The Grimkés, like all the really fanatical Abolitionists, were essentially vicious. Their freedom from the blatantly mercenary spirit, prevalent in their day as in ours, diverted attention from the vice that did permeate them. There is a form of avarice that often goes unrecognized because it does not fix its desire on gold; but the lust for power may be as sordid a thing as the lust for money. Even the moment that is generally accounted heroic, that in which the Grimkés acknowledged their Negro nephew, was forced upon them. They had not troubled to inform themselves of the boy's existence until by his own efforts he began to attract public attention; and after that it was hopeless to attempt to conceal his origin.

Their basic attitude toward Negroes was revealed by their perfectly genuine horror when they discovered the existence of Negro relatives. Theirs was precisely the emotional state of many a modern liberal who finds himself being twice as polite to a Negro as he would be to a white man under similar circumstances; he is over-compensating for his lack of any genuine rapport with the man. What the liberal feels is what the Grimkés felt, not love of the Negro, but hatred of those who oppress him.

Hatred of oppression is incontestably a noble emotion, but hatred of oppressors is questionable. They should be stripped of their power to oppress and some, perhaps, should be hanged as a warning to others who might be tempted to imitate them; but these operations should be conducted coldly and with no touch of exultation. They never are. Fallible humanity cannot rise to such heights. But fallible humanity can make some progress toward them, and a man who obviously luxuriates in his hatred of oppressors is below the level attainable and attained by civilized people. Such a man, people say, is possessed by the mob spirit.

The fact that the Abolitionists were frequently victims of the mob is simply a demonstration that action and reaction are equal and opposite. They denied the right of anyone else to hold an opinion contrary to their own. Rejection of their opinion was proof of moral turpitude. This is precisely the spirit of the mob. The Grimkés consistently and persistently incited the mob spirit and in so doing they, proclaiming and undoubtedly believing themselves protagonists of human freedom, were in fact enemies of liberty.

This bitter indictment would seem to preclude the possibility of finding in the story any support for the original thesis of this study, namely, that great influence in a free society is invariably based on some quality whose social value is real and solid. But it is an error, based on the widely accepted superstition that enemies of liberty are by definition valueless people. Dr. Samuel Johnson was an avowed and vociferous enemy of political, and contemptuous of religious freedom; but would anyone seriously contend that he was of no value to society?

Dr. Johnson greatly advanced the cause he professed to oppose merely by boldly proclaiming what he believed to be true although nobody knew better than he that "thrift may follow fawning." By being himself he demonstrated the value of the individual which is the philosophic basis of liberty. So the Grimkés, by being themselves in the teeth of violent opposition, compelled a reluctant admiration and inspired in others determination also to be free.

One may view their ends with indifference and their motives with distaste, but that does not alter the fact that the individual who will neither cringe nor pose, but stands for what he is without apology or pretense, breaks the way for others. The result is not necessarily happy—Al Capone broke open the way to gangsterism for many others, just as surely as Abraham Lincoln broke open the way to liberty, not merely for American slaves but for millions in far corners of the world. Similarly the Grimkés helped clear the way for the Claflin sisters as well as for Jane Addams; but they undoubtedly did much to break open the way to liberty for American women.

They were free spirits, and every free spirit is an addition to the wealth of the nation; for long after their follies have evaporated, and their mistakes have been rectified, their stand for liberty will be remembered and will give heart to others who suffer under oppression. So generations later men who wish to be free have cause to be thankful that they lived.

5

proem

Came, to adopt the remarkable style of the movies and Time *magazine, the dawn. The lapse of interest in general ideas that attended the Era of Good Feeling (an era, incidentally, of as poisonous personal hatreds and of as industrious back-stabbing as American politics ever knew) could not last. The Era of Good Feeling is considered to have extended over two administrations, the second of James Monroe and the only of John Quincy Adams. Then arrived Andrew Jackson, magnificently innocent of good feeling, but marvelously equipped to arouse the emotions of the common man and spur him to frenzied activity.*

Intense emotionalism may not lead to cerebration in the common man, but it certainly makes others think. The terror of Nicholas Biddle and his friends undoubtedly spurred their mental activities, and by the time the Jacksonian regime ended with the defeat of Van Buren in 1840 it was not characteristic of any prominent American to be at ease in Zion. True, the vigorous search was no longer for the meaning of life and the place of man in the cosmos, the theme of the remarkable correspondence between Jefferson and Adams, but it was a search for ideas.

This once more opened the gates of opportunity to thinkers— not political philosophers of the old type, but nevertheless thinkers—and they came swarming in.

As witness the following tale of:

HORACE GREELEY

who had ideas when they were needed

THE REVEREND JOSEPH BUSHNELL Grinnell lost his voice. It was a catastrophe for a rising young clergyman in the days when electronic amplifiers had not yet been invented and when even Congregational clergymen depended largely upon eloquence for their effect. But, like Falstaff who was the cause that wit was in other men, Joseph Grinnell, speechless, was the cause of one of the most famous utterances in the history of the United States. That utterance was, "Go west, young man, go west."

For Grinnell in his perplexity asked advice of Horace Greeley, editor of the New York *Tribune*. It was the conventional thing to do. Everyone, in any perplexity, asked advice of Horace Greeley and none failed to receive it. It was satisfactory advice, too, because it was forthright, flat and firm. The less Greeley knew about the subject, the less compromising he was in discussing it. He had learned one of the great secrets of manipulating public opinion, which is, on matters with which you are familiar be cautious, but when you don't know what you are talking about be dogmatic. As between alternatives, in the "either-or" situation, no matter which side you take there is a fifty-fifty chance that you will be right; when you are right people will remember it with an admiration approaching awe, whereas when you are wrong it is likely soon to be forgotten. So many people are wrong that one more makes little difference; but so few people are certain that when one is both certain and right he is very conspicuous.

In the case of Grinnell, for instance, Greeley was right. The young man went to Iowa, subordinated theology to law and politics, founded the town of Grinnell and the institution that later became Grinnell College, built railroads, went to Congress, became a famous Abolitionist, and introduced superior cattle and horses into Iowa. In short, by following Greeley's advice he lived long and prospered. Thousands of others, following the same advice, starved, whipped by grasshoppers and drought, and are forgotten, but Grinnell is remembered. One such instance is enough to establish oracular authority and Horace Greeley scored many equivalent successes. As a result he attained a position in American life that has no close parallel a hundred years later and that cannot be understood by modern Americans as long as they confine their inquiries to the written record.

For on the face of the record Horace Greeley was just about the giddiest old goat that ever played a prominent role in public affairs. He plunged headlong into every fad that the times produced. He was a food faddist, a dress faddist, a religious faddist, an economic faddist. He was enchanted by Margaret Fuller, the Feminist, Sylvester Graham, the dietician, and François Marie Charles Fourier, the social reformer; and his enthusiastic advocacy was such that it is hard to say whether he thought the fate of the world hinged more on Women's Rights, graham bread, or the organization of society into phalansteries. Like many successful journalists he found the business of merely interpreting politics begin to pall on him and yielded to the temptation to dabble actively in the art; and, like most journalists who have yielded to the temptation, he was a fabulously bad politician.

Nevertheless, Greeley in his time was a great man, and of all the conspicuous members of the Lunatic Fringe he, who was most completely devoid of common sense, enjoys the best reputation for hardheaded realism. Here, obviously, is a mystery and it can be penetrated only by turning away from Greeley himself and examining the intellectual climate of the country during his lifetime.

The kind of instruction in history that came down from Suetonius, who wrote of the Twelve Caesars mentioning the rest of Rome only incidentally, prevailed in this country until quite recently, giving schoolboys of the last generation a firm conviction that from the War of 1812 to the Civil War nothing happened in this country except the Mexican War. The truth is, of course, that it was precisely in this period that everything happened—that is to say, everything that had an important influence on the subsequent development of the nation.

But the most significant changes that took place were not effected by either military or political campaigns. They were changes in attitudes and habits of thought, which are not taken down by secretaries and filed in official documents, hence are not readily available to historians working exclusively in official archives. Not until John Bach McMaster had the brilliant inspiration that a contemporary newspaper might tell more than a minute-book does about what happened did we begin to get away from the delusion that in the United States from 1815 to 1860 about the only thing worth mentioning was Old Fuss-and-Feathers' campaign from Vera Cruz to Chapultepec.

Yet this was the period that saw the obliteration of the last remnants of colonialism with its overtones of monarchy and caste. On July 4, 1826, Thomas Jefferson and John Adams both died, each to the very end entertaining a suspicion, Jefferson with revulsion, Adams with a touch of nostalgia, that the revival of monarchy in America was conceivable. But by July 4, 1826, the country's dominant political leaders were Henry Clay and John C. Calhoun, with

Daniel Webster coming up fast. Clay was born in 1777, Calhoun and Webster in 1782, which is to say none of the three had lived as a loyal subject of a king, or had any suspicion that he ever would or could. They could not regard restoration of kingship as an idea to be taken seriously.

In this they were representative of the population. The generation that had fought the Revolution was gone and its mental attitudes and habits with it. There were still vestigial remainders of the caste system, notably the institution of Negro slavery, but the faith that social orders were ordained of God was definitely shattered and could never be restored. The trend was all in the other direction and by the end of the period not even as strongly intrenched a caste institution as slavery could stand against the increasing pressure toward legal and political equality.

But if Americans of that day were firmly and finally convinced that the old order was dead, they were sharply and at times uncomfortably aware that the new one was still struggling to be born. They were assured that a great change had taken place, but they could say with the Evangelist, "it doth not yet appear what we shall be." In such circumstances any man with an idea is certain to obtain a hearing, and the more novel the idea, the better; for the only certainty is that the old notions have failed.

Great hospitality to ideas in times of stress is a phenomenon familiar enough. We have seen it on a colossal scale twice since 1776—in the French and again in the Russian revolutions. The peculiarity of the American situation was the relative absence of fear. After the fighting stopped in 1781 there were thirty years of military quiet, and after 1815 thirty years more. Revolutions always release not the philosophers only, but also the bedlamites, and if the revolution is in desperate fear the wild men receive a measure of attention that would not be given them by a people unblinded by terror. After Yorktown the American revolutionists felt fairly secure from the military standpoint; so although the ferment of thought tossed up in this country figures every whit as fantastic as Anacharsis Clootz or N. I. Bukharin, they never obtained such influence here as they did in France and Russia.

Horace Greeley, of course, was never in the same category as Clootz and Bukharin, but he gave assistance to some men who were—Fourier and Graham, for example. Yet he commanded the respectful attention of thousands of Americans who were not only sane but notably hardheaded realists. This is not in fact the contradiction that it seems. America was striking out on a new course and all realists knew it. In such a situation the urgent demand is for new ideas and it is realism to seek them. Horace Greeley was full of ideas, and if some of them were fantastic, others were not. "Go west, young man," was, on the whole, excellent advice. Furthermore, Greeley could express an idea pungently and clearly. A man who constantly offered pungent, clear ideas, some good, was to be preferred to a man with no ideas at all; for the one sure way for the new country to ruin itself would be to fail to do any fresh thinking.

The influence that Greeley attained and held for thirty years was based on a sound instinct in the American people. If it seems strange today, one may not blink the fact that a possible explanation is that the people have lost that sound instinct in the course of a hundred years. Greeley at his nuttiest was bold and original; and in consideration of those two qualities his contemporaries excused his follies. The modern generation seems to have been persuaded, at least to a large extent, that bold and original thinking in politics is subversive and ought to be suppressed; which is probably more lunatic than anything that Greeley ever advocated.

In the pre-Civil War period three names dominate the his-

tory of American journalism so completely that even a hint
of criticism of their professional competence is shocking; yet
it can be argued plausibly that all of them survived, and two
of them survived only, by their possession of boldness and
originality. These *grands seigneurs* of the craft were Greeley,
Dana and Bennett, but as journalists are measured now Bennett was the only great newspaperman in the lot. Greeley
and Dana were fine editors, indeed great editors, but Dana
was an indifferent publisher and in that capacity Greeley was
definitely incompetent. He went broke twice before he
achieved a large, if temporary, success with the *Tribune,* and
before the end of his life he had lost even that. Bennett
alone passed on a going and highly profitable concern to his
heirs.

Yet it is a safe assertion that if any half-dozen modern news-
papermen, taken at random, were asked to rate Greeley, Dana
and Bennett in order of professional competence, five of the
six would put Bennett at the bottom of the list. The craft
simply does not, will not, and cannot rate brilliance in the
business office on as high a level as brilliance in the editorial
rooms. Even power is not accepted as the *summum bonum*
by this curious fraternity. Bennett had power enough to
compel Abraham Lincoln to knuckle under on more than
one occasion, but that is not enough to make him the newspaperman's newspaperman. That position is held by Dana,
with Greeley probably in second place.

With the general public, including the Faculty of History,
Greeley undoubtedly leads. His position is probably affected by moralistic overtones. Bennett and Dana were both
pretty rascally in some of their dealings and the American
public is irrevocably committed to the view that conceding
greatness to a rogue is, as Mark Twain said of calling Her-
cules a demigod, unconstitutional. Greeley, on the other
hand, consistently practiced all the conventional virtues ex-

cept orthodox church membership. He represented his time. Even in his eccentricities he was eccentric in a way that his contemporaries could easily understand. Therefore he gained an ascendancy equalled by no other journalist in our history, Benjamin Franklin alone excepted, and it has continued into our day.

He was born in 1811 of old and exhausted New England stock in Amherst, New Hampshire. The original Greeley landed in this country in 1670, and the second and third generations had done pretty well, but the fourth was not much and the fifth—represented by Zaccheus Greeley, Horace's father—had utterly run to seed. It was not that there was anything vicious in Zac; it was merely that he was too spiritless to summon up energy enough even for vice, other than the rather passive vice of getting liquored up too frequently.

Zac Greeley very likely would have ended his days in the poorhouse except for his marriage. Mary Woodburn was also of old American stock, but in her the peasant blood ran strong, and she would not succumb. She not only bore and raised a houseful of children and did the work of a field hand, especially at harvest time, but she undoubtedly spurred Zac to efforts that he never would have made alone. She gave him at least the impetus to move after his successive failures. The family trailed slowly across New York state and finally into Pennsylvania, then frontier country.

Her second and oldest surviving child, Horace, never doubted that from his mother he inherited what driving force he had. It was not altogether a matter of genes, it was environment too. Horace was the weakling of the flock and, as often happens with a strong mother, this one got more than an equal share of maternal attention and affection. The boy was not quite what country people then called "afflicted," but he was physically abnormal. His eyes were weak from childhood and he developed a spindly frame with a disproportionately large head.

Obviously, he was ill-equipped for the battle of life on a backwoods farm, where physical strength and good co-ordination are of prime importance. Mary realized when he was quite small that he would have to rely on that big head rather than on those pipestem arms and legs to make his way in the world and, wisely, she did everything she could to develop his intellectual capacity. Judged by modern educational standards it was not much, but it was a start and it was enough. She taught him to read almost by the time he could walk. He learned to read standing at her knee while she held an open book on her lap and in this way the boy developed ability to follow a line of type upside down, or sidewise, as readily as from the conventional position—an accomplishment that assisted him no little when he took up the printer's trade, for printers habitually read type upside down because in that way they can follow it from left to right. Reading a line upside down is much easier than reading one from right to left.

Horace developed into an omnivorous reader and such a phenomenal speller that by the time he was nine certain neighbors who were men of substance offered to club together and pay for his education at Exeter Academy, but his mother objected. She was probably right. A boy of nine who was a physical oddity very likely needed maternal care much more than he needed intellectual discipline.

But at fifteen, when his luckless father was contemplating the family's final move, Horace took his future into his own hands. Instead of trailing along with the rest into Pennsylvania, he went the other way. He tramped twelve miles to East Poultney, Vermont, and there opened negotiations for his own apprenticeship to the local printer. His father agreed, and this time Mary raised no objection. So Greeley came into journalism by the avenue of the type-case.

Among the printers he became noted, says his latest biographer,* for two characteristics—a voracious appetite and a loquacity that matched his remarkable feats as a trencherman. If he talked incessantly, though, he talked well. At least East Poultney thought so, for this odd-looking youth read every newspaper he could lay hands on and remembered what he read. He was without question the best-informed individual in the village, and the farmers frequenting the local inn where he lived found him a mine of information on current events.

Hale argues convincingly that this garrulity was a case of over-compensation. In whatever involved physical strength and agility Greeley was at a hopeless disadvantage, but conversation was one activity in which he could shine, and he made the most of it. This seems probably true, but it was not all. The kind of mind that takes a man into journalism is one with a strong, not to say ruling passion for getting people told. Why else spend one's life handling the news? Greeley doubtless felt a normal desire to excel in something, but in his case it reinforced a natural bent, and probably doubled his output of words. Be that as it may, in these years he talked about everything and, in the absence of evidence to the contrary, we may suppose that he ate everything. There is no suggestion in the record that the youth was given to dietary fads.

What he did not do, as everyone remembered, was drink— spruce beer, yes, and homemade wines, but in the early years of the nineteenth century nothing less potent than whisky

---

* Hale, William Harlan, *Horace Greeley, Voice of the People,* 1950. James Parton, the universal biographer, wrote up Greeley as a matter of course, and so did L. D. Ingersoll (1873) and W. A. Linn (1903); special aspects of his career have been treated by half a dozen others. But for the modern reader Hale's is decidedly the best book on the subject.

or brandy was considered a drink. The reason for the boy's abstinence is not far to seek. Zac Greeley had been what we would now describe as an alcoholic, and even Mary did not hesitate to take a pull at the jug when it was passed around in the hayfield. Perhaps they drank because they lived a hard life, but their son was convinced that they lived a hard life because they drank, and at the age of thirteen he "took the pledge." What is far more noteworthy is that he kept it the rest of his life.

Greeley apparently did not quite serve out his apprenticeship, but through no fault of his own. Just before his time was up the printing business that employed him failed. His articles provided that if he served full time he was to have forty dollars in clothing, but since he did not serve full time, and since his employer was bankrupt, he was apparently content to settle for a secondhand overcoat.

He left Vermont to go to the rescue of his family, making heavy weather of the pioneer life in the wilds of Erie County, Pennsylvania. But Horace's help was not too effective, for there was not much work for a printer in the backwoods. In any event, Zac and Mary had another son and two daughters, all of whom were much better adapted to pioneer conditions than Horace was, so after a year or two he made the final break. He had saved twenty-five dollars; half of it he gave to his father and with the other half set out for New York, fame, and fortune.

His first few months in New York were pretty rough, but Horace had the energy and resolution that his father lacked. Within two years he had managed to become a partner in a small print shop. Within another year he and his partner were publishing a penny daily, the *Morning Post,* that failed rapidly. A year after that he had his own weekly magazine, the *New Yorker,* that made the grade, but without any large success. In the meantime, three printers and a reporter, sitting around a table in a Park Row tavern, made up their minds that the idea of the *Morning Post* had been all right, and that Greeley failed only because he mishandled it. One of the printers was Ben Day, and the reporter was James Gordon Bennett. Day, more to advertise his job-printing business than for anything else, set up a penny paper called the *Sun,* and instantly began to coin money. At that, Bennett, with equipment consisting, according to his own account, of a plank laid across two barrels, set up the New York *Herald,* and he too was instantly successful.

The other two printers, A. S. Abell and William M. Swain, feeling, to their chagrin, that Day and Bennett had stolen the New York field, departed, first to set up the *Public Ledger* in Philadelphia, and later the *Sun,* in Baltimore. Among them these four newspapers worked a revolution in American journalism; but it was Greeley's abortive *Morning Post* that started the movement.

For several years Greeley merely watched others reap where he had sown. In 1838 his magazine was doing so poorly that he was glad to accept a thousand dollars from Thurlow Weed, the Whig boss of New York, to edit a campaign sheet from Albany, spending half the week there and the other half in New York City getting out the *New Yorker.* In 1840, a Presidential year, he made a similar arrangement, but this time William H. Seward, as well as Weed, was in on the deal. Greeley did a good job with the publication, called the *Log Cabin,* but he was not happy working under two bosses, especially such exacting ones as Seward and Weed.

But the enterprise did allow him to accumulate a little capital with which, in 1841, he plunged into the penny daily field with a paper called the *Tribune.* Its instant and tremendous success is journalistic history too well known to justify repetition here.

In the meantime he had made a marriage which by common consent is regarded as a disaster, as indeed it was from every conventional point of view. Mary Cheney was as eccentric as Greeley himself. Margaret Fuller described her as "a typical Yankee schoolmistress" which is hard on the Yankee schoolmistress but does convey an idea. The very fact that when she came to New York she chose to live in Dr. Sylvester Graham's boardinghouse is sufficient evidence of her deviation from the normal, for the fare was not only vegetarian but was prepared without condiments; salt, pepper, vinegar, mustard and the rest were denied the perfectly healthy, not merely those suffering from some abnormal condition. His insistence upon the dietetic value of whole-wheat bread has preserved Graham's name and also obscured a vast amount of fol-de-rol that he practiced, for he was one of the most extravagant quacks in our history.

One may argue that all of Dr. Graham's boarders must have been suffering from some abnormal condition, or they would not have been there. The point has a certain merit, but the abnormality was psychological, rather than physiological. Mary Cheney, for example, obviously deviated from the norm, but there is not the slightest evidence that there was anything wrong with her digestive system when she was a young woman.

Apparently she was simply one of those persons—always a minority, but always a very considerable minority to the woe of the world—who are afflicted with immutable moral certainties about everything. Early in life Mary made up her mind about what the universe should be, and when she found it different it never occurred to her to question her own postulates; she simply denounced the universe. For instance, Horace held that a woman is only a woman, but a newspaper is a job, and a job requires attention ahead of any woman. This Mary never admitted and with her romantic and highly unrealistic view of the relation of the sexes probably could not admit; so she made her husband's life a hell on earth.

The conventional comment on this is that they should never have married. Perhaps the conventional view is correct, but it is open to certain objections. Who but Mary Cheney would ever have married Horace Greeley? Who but Horace would ever have married Mary Cheney? He was far from handsome, she was far from pretty. He was dogmatic, she was supercilious. He had none of the social graces, she was too superior to stoop to such frivolity. Both were intellectual, but to say that either was intelligent is to put a pretty severe strain on the definition of the word.

But they were both human beings, and it was his professional aim to exercise influence upon large numbers of other people. A man who assumes to instruct and advise others about their worldly affairs, but who has no personal experience of the institution of marriage, is in a questionable position. Domestic cares and domestic unhappiness are so tremendous a factor in human existence that a man who knows nothing of either cannot know much about people. So to assert that Greeley's marriage was utter disaster is to assume a great deal; it probably did something to humanize him and he was a man in conspicuous need of humanizing. As for Mary, marriage gave her a life of physical comfort and leisure to bemoan her ills and slights. So the theory that assuming the holy bonds meant more loss than gain to either is debatable and must remain so until our ability to measure the effect of psychological stresses and strains is far greater than it is now, or seems likely ever to be.

In any event it is of record that Horace Greeley gained a position of enormous influence while arguing for as odd a set of "reforms" as any famous American ever supported. He was against meat, white bread, pepper, salt, coffee and tea, as well as tobacco and distilled spirits. He was in favor of the emancipation of women and Negroes, but against war to effect either freedom; yet when war came his agitation for fast and furious war did much to drive the Federal government into the precipitate action that culminated in the disaster at Bull Run. He gave Margaret Fuller a forum in which to proclaim the unpopular doctrine of Women's Rights. He gave space to the unpopular Abolitionists. He gave space to the followers of Fourier to advertise their peculiar brand of socialism. He hired Dana, a former denizen of Brook Farm, and made him his chief aide. After the Civil War when Jefferson Davis had lain in jail for two years without trial, Greeley signed his bail bond. Finally, he ran for President against the national hero, General Grant.

In brief, Greeley supported practically every unpopular cause that attracted attention in his day, yet he was popular. Up to the moment when he performed the most thoroughly decent act of his career, signing the Davis bail bond, he was immensely popular. Since men do not attain popularity by championing unpopular causes it is evident that some other factor operated in Greeley's case; and that factor probably reveals more about the country than it does about the man.

Certain negatives are immediately apparent. Greeley's success was not won by brilliance. Dana and Godkin were far better newspaper writers and Bennett was a better phrasemaker. In fact, Greeley's only good one, his campaign slogan in 1872, "Turn the rascals out!" was coined by Dana. Nearly everything the famous editor wrote makes dull reading today, and "Go west, young man," is the only flashing phrase of his that is still remembered.

He did not succeed by the favor of a patron. His alliance with Weed and Seward in 1840 did give him the small amount of capital required to launch the *Tribune,* but thereafter it was the politicians who sought Greeley's favor, not he who sought theirs. As for advertising, it was still in its infancy as the financial support of journalism. Greeley did not even court the favor of his readers by any truckling to their prejudices; on the contrary, he was constantly startling and sometimes outraging them.

One source of his strength was his transparent honesty, but to assume that this was the chief source is to ignore the fact that at the same time and place others, notably Dana and Bennett, were hugely successful without being overburdened with honesty. There must have been other factors strongly influencing this man's career.

Two come to mind immediately—breadth of view and intellectual curiosity. The editorial page of the *Tribune* was not parochial, especially the editorial page of the weekly edition circulated outside of New York City. It was through the weekly that Greeley spoke to the nation precisely at the moment when the parochialism of the thirteen colonies was yielding place to a continental point of view. Greeley was one editor who could visualize Minnesota as well as Manhattan; and this harmonized with the growing vision of the people.

The second characteristic, hospitality to ideas, was not monopolized by Greeley. Bennett, in particular, exhibited intellectual curiosity in a high degree, and prospered thereby, for it was consonant with the mood of the people. They were taking over an empty continent, an experience without precedent within the memory of any civilized nation. So the problems they faced were new problems, requiring new solutions; and it was natural that any man with new ideas, including Bennett, would attract much attention.

But Bennett's impact upon the times did not compare with Greeley's because Bennett was incurably frivolous, or at least bore that reputation, and a genuine oracle must be humorless. Cicero could not understand how one augur could meet another without smiling, but that was because Cicero was not an augur; the true haruspex was the Red Queen, who could believe as many as six impossible things before breakfast. Greeley qualified. A touch of humor would have made him a happier man and a wiser man, but it is far from certain that it would have made him a more influential man. It might have made him a weaker one.

He spoke solemnly and as one having authority to a people avid of authoritative information. In the period of Greeley's greatest influence, the thirty years following the founding of the *Tribune* in 1841, the American people felt a thirst for ideas raging beyond anything else of the kind in their history. The most convincing proof of this is to be found, not in their eulogists, but in those who satirized them. Consider, for example, the blistering American episode in *Martin Chuzzlewit*. Dickens at his most venomous nevertheless pictured a community strangely reminiscent of Saint Paul's description of the Athenians of his day who "spent their time in nothing else, but either to tell, or to hear some new thing."

It was inevitable. Geographically, the country was expanding at a rate that resembled explosion more than expansion. By 1846 the jurisdiction of the United States had reached the Pacific, but administration and exploitation were far behind jurisdiction. A new situation was created, one in which precedents were few and those few for the most part unreliable; obviously the crying need was for ideas, the more novel the better. Repeated failure had not yet made us chary of novelty, even in the more thickly settled East; and repeated success had filled us with the heady belief that in America nothing was impossible.

Naturally, it was a happy hunting ground for fakers and frauds of every imaginable stripe, which was the aspect of it that struck Dickens and many other foreign observers; only occasionally did a De Tocqueville perceive that the very gaudiness of the swindlers and scoundrels was evidence of an astounding hospitality to ideas signalizing an intellectual expansion comparable to the country's geographical extension.

But it was so. The intellectual ferment in the United States in this period was prodigious, but it has been obscured by the fact that it issued in physical action rather than in the formulation of philosophies. The creation of an elaborate system of thought commands the respectful attention of intellectuals; but they are reluctant to admit that the creation of an elaborate system of railways is the result of cerebration as bold and original as anything achieved by Aristotle, or Descartes, or Marx.

A hundred years later the intellectual climate is so different that a great effort of imagination is required to understand the effect when a man bubbling with ideas spoke to a population not yet afraid of ideas but, on the contrary, feeling a great need of them. There were, of course, exceptions. Between 1841 and 1872 the United States had elements that shuddered at every new concept, among them one great economic interest, slavery, determined to throttle innovation by force if necessary. But these elements were not dominant, and the chief of the powers of reaction, the Peculiar Institution, labored under the handicap of being attainted by the moral condemnation of mankind. In general, Americans were eager to hear and to consider any suggestion for the betterment of the economic, the political, or the social system.

Needless to say, they were victimized by many swindlers and by even more crackpots, but they also profited by much good and some inspired leadership. In retrospect, of course, the quacks and the rogues stand out because their operations were spectacular. Some of them, indeed, beggared description. Dickens' fictional Eden Land Corporation is a dull and lifeless thing by comparison with the actual, real-life operations of such characters as Uncle Dan Drew and Jim Fiske. The honest visionaries, too, frequently produced effects as gaudy as any of the bedizened rascals. Brook Farm and the other phalansteries, Oneida, New Harmony and a dozen others are unforgettable; and above all the early days of the great Mormon movement wrote into our national history one of its most colorful chapters.

But to be victimized is the occupational risk of any people

who are engaged in pushing back their intellectual horizons. In the case of the United States it didn't matter a great deal. This is the all-important point. This very generation, gulled as people have seldom been gulled in history, nevertheless mastered a continent and laid the foundations of a colossal political and economic structure. In the flood of ideas that they welcomed joyously, so many were good that they overcompensated for the villainous and the idiotic and the country flourished prodigiously.

It is hard to believe that a new Horace Greeley today could survive his own eccentricities, but this is no guarantee that the mental health of the country has improved. With the creation of great wealth and power we have acquired great caution with regard to novelty. Our fear of losing what we have has chilled our hope of attaining the heart's desire. So we regard with dark suspicion the leader who turns eagerly to the new and untried. We find great difficulty in conceiving of him as the herald of a new dawn; it is much easier to view him as an emissary of the Prince of the Powers of Darkness. This represents a slowing down, doubtless inevitable as a country grows rich and powerful, but probably no occasion for congratulation and certainly no occasion for boasting.

In the mid-twentieth century a new Horace Greeley could hardly edit a new *Tribune*. He would not have time. He would be too busy responding to the subpoenas of Congressional investigating committees and defending himself against the assault of professional patrioteers. In the twentieth century we have developed the weird delusion that all new ideas originate in Moscow, and the man who propounds one is to be regarded as an agent of the communists until proved innocent. So today there is evidence that, in spite of our wealth and power, we are losing the leadership of the world as fast as, in spite of our poverty and relative impotence, we were gaining it in Greeley's time.

What the man taught, reduced to its essence, was confidence. But it was confidence in the mass, not in individuals. Greeley never propagated the theory of the Big Brother, or of the Great White Father. He did not share the delusion that betrayed millions into blind faith in a Hitler, a Stalin, a Roosevelt, an Eisenhower, as the indispensable leader who alone could save the country. For one reason, he knew too many leaders too well. In the beginning of his career he was closely associated with Weed and Seward, and later he knew them all, including Lincoln; and he knew that the genius of the nation is not embodied in any one man.

But he did believe in the existence of that genius. What is more to the point, so did the majority of his readers. It was not then regarded as mysticism to believe that in the mass of the people there is a wisdom that, fallible as it is in detail, on issues of the widest scope is superior to the wisdom of any individual no matter how brilliant. Generations before the term emergent evolution had been coined, Americans had somehow adumbrated the idea that organization itself is an entity and that an organization is greater than the sum of its parts.

All the Americans of Greeley's generation had long been dead before such non-conformists as Bergson and Heard began to fumble for the meaning of the observed fact that the swarm is greater than the individual bee multiplied by 100,-000, or whatever the number of bees in the hive. Yet those long-gone Americans knew it. They could be utterly realistic about the capacity of any specimen under direct observation and yet cherish a tremendous faith in the aggregate. To the marrow of their bones they were convinced that a great nation could be built out of some millions of Sad Sacks.

The insanity of this belief would be certifiable except for the disconcerting fact that the thing was done. The United States did become a great nation. For a long time the official, i.e., the pedagogical, explanation was that we were blessed with a series of demigods who did the work in spite of the

stupidity and instability of the people. Up to Greeley's time
these supermen included Washington, Jefferson, Hamilton,
Jackson and Lincoln; but subsequent investigation has revealed that all of them were made of remarkably common
clay. All were men of extraordinary ability, of course, but
none was free of the frailties and follies that are common to
humanity.

Yet the nation grew wealthy and powerful beyond all precedent without any conspicuous rise in either the moral or
the intellectual level of the typical American. The true explanation seems to lie in what Woodrow Wilson would have
called the release of the generous energies of the people. This
the American system did accomplish with conspicuous, nay,
spectacular success; and an important reason for its success
was its extreme hospitality to ideas.

No doubt a majority of the ideas it welcomed was idiotic,
but a saving remnant was sound. The idiocies were tran-
sient and the damage they did was repaired, usually fairly
soon; but the true discoveries in the art of government were
permanent, and on them the success of the republic was based.

Greeley's value to the nation was his leadership in the dis-
semination of ideas. For years his managing editor was
Charles A. Dana, and after him Whitelaw Reid, neither of
whom shrank from an idea because it was new. Greeley himself hired Margaret Fuller and bought articles from Henry
George. Dana employed as a regular correspondent from
London a caustic economist named Karl Marx, and, apparently without consulting Greeley, employed John Hay as an
editorial writer. The inevitable result of this galaxy of tal-
ent was that the boys were constantly putting over something
that the Old Man did not like; but he tolerated it because
he preferred ideas to conformity.

Toward the end he began to slip and for the last few years
the paper was more Whitelaw Reid's than Greeley's. His
slipshod financial methods eventually lost him control of all

but a minority interest and at his death the *Tribune* was the property of others. Yet "slipshod" is an ungenerous word. Greeley's ruin was not carelessness so much as undue generosity to both friends and causes that interested him. He was a proverbially easy victim for any hard-luck story and a constant subscriber to projects for the public, but not for private benefit. He was the least mercenary of men and mere possession of wealth did not interest him.

His end was startling, but characteristic. Sickened by the abominable record of the first Grant administration, both in its financial corruption and in its deliberate fomenting of hate for partisan profit, he joined other liberal Republicans in putting a third ticket in the field. As it turned out, it was only a second ticket, for the Democrats, shattered by the aftermath of the war and under the wildly impractical leadership of another editor, Henry Watterson, indorsed Greeley and put up no ticket of their own.

At the start the idea seemed logical, for Grant had been woefully disappointing—not surprising, since he had been elected in a burst of sentimentality, not because he was a statesman, but because he was a national hero. In the circumstances the opposition should have chosen a candidate who unquestionably was a statesman and one of demonstrated capacity. Charles Francis Adams probably would have been the best choice, but in a long series of worse than dubious political deals he was thrust aside and Greeley was persuaded to take the nomination.

Of all his aberrations, this was by far the most irrational. Sensible men, aware that Grant was a bad President, yet feared that Greeley would be many times worse; and the unthinking deemed it presumptuous for a mere newspaper editor to contend against the man who had won the war. Greeley went down to catastrophic defeat, and the thieves and merchants of hate were assured of another four years of power.

It was too much. Never physically strong, Greeley wore himself out in the fantastic campaign and when the results were known he collapsed, mentally and physically. He was removed to a nursing home where he died on November 29, 1872, just three weeks after the election.

Horace Greeley's pre-eminence in the Lunatic Fringe is unquestionable, yet it is equally unquestionable that he was a powerful and valuable man. The question is, what was the element in his make-up that was so valuable as to make his lunacies relatively trivial? It is not far to seek. It was his complete freedom from the fear of taking the next step that hampers and often hamstrings men whose intellectual capacity is at least equal to his.

In addition, he had the advantage of living in a period when this fear happened to be at a low ebb among the American people. It was a period of brisk confidence before demagogues, serving their own purposes, had inoculated us with the fear of intelligence that became so conspicuous in the middle years of the twentieth century. The timidity of great wealth had not yet become dominant in the country; there were rich men even then, but little evidence of the *rentier* psychology appeared among them. The great majority had made their own fortunes by bold and vigorous action, so they naturally looked upon boldness and vigor with much more favor than do those who have inherited their money, and whose fear of losing it is dominant because they lack faith in their capacity to make more.

So Greeley was well received because he was a child of the age. Let us not deny him due credit. He had honesty, courage, and intellectual alertness. He was a disinterested patriot. But with all these he would have made no such impression on history had he not been the right man living at the right time.

6

proem

The economic and political changes in the United States from the reign of Andrew Jackson on were too obvious to be ignored, but the change in social attitudes, no less profound, went unacknowledged, for the most part, by the pontifices who ruled society and whose decretals usually went unquestioned by a submissive press.

Nevertheless, a crisis was building up. Under pioneer conditions the division of labor as between the sexes is sharply defined, and with it their respective spheres of influence. The pioneer woman is always subjected to hardship and usually to heavy labor; but that she is oppressed is not true at all. On the American frontier the dominance of the female within the walls of the home was commonplace. For one reason, the frontier woman had scarcity value; her man, knowing that she would be hard to replace, could not afford to tyrannize without limit, and the severity of the pioneer's struggle for survival forbade much intramural bickering.

But as the struggle for survival eased off the position of women deteriorated. A generation after the second war with Great Britain their status had come pretty close to villein socage, not to say chattel slavery, and the daughters of the pioneer women were becoming more and more restive under it. Their mothers and grandmothers had been powerful and free, in fact if not in law, and the memory lingered among women whom a rigid social sys-

*tem was reducing closer and closer to purdah, the Hindu system
of seclusion of women.*

*But the lords of creation were as a rule oblivious of the mount-
ing pressure, and when it occasionally burst all bounds they were
quite genuinely shocked and scandalized. This gave rise to many
of the sensations and broad farces of the time.*

In witness whereof, let us now give attention to the tale of:

VICTORIA CLAFLIN WOODHULL

who yielded no precedence to Phryne

MRS. JOHN BIDDULPH MARTIN, widow of a rich English banker and sister of the Marchioness of Montserrat, lived
to the ripe old age of eighty-nine, and in 1927 died in the
odor of sanctity, much esteemed for her charitable works.
Which was a scandal in the eyes of those who esteemed themselves as right-thinkers, for this estimable matron had once
borne the terrific name of Victoria Claflin Woodhull.

It was the belief of the righteous, which they had done
their best to translate into action, that she should have been
dressed in a yellow robe and incinerated in an auto-da-fé attended by the clergy, the nobility and the gentry. It was not
merely that her adulteries had been numerous and notorious.
Many a great lady before and after her time has been dis-
dainful of her lawful marriage bed with impunity. It was not
merely that she was a blackmailer. Many a sanctified enterprise—the Prohibition Amendment, for a conspicuous
example—has been rammed through Congress and state
legislatures by methods that were moral, if not legal blackmail. It was not merely that she was a spectacularly successful swindler. Swindlers even more conscienceless have been

rewarded with seats in the United States Senate.

Her crime was more heinous than any of these, or than all of them put together. She attacked and seriously damaged several of our most pompous and venerated frauds, including the double moral standard, the legal ascendancy of the male, and Pecksniffian religion. In doing this she made monkeys out of Senators, bankers, editors and eloquent divines; and whoso makes monkeys out of our popular idols inevitably makes the idolaters look simian. The crime of Benedict Arnold was a mere peccadillo by comparison with the offense of one who makes the American fool see himself for a fool. This woman made vast numbers of the self-righteous appear silly in their own eyes; she was unspeakable.

And yet there was in her career a certain adherence to basic truth that commands the admiration of realists, accompanied by a flouting of all the laws of probability that delights artists. As John Steinbeck said of Joan of Arc, her story fascinates us because it "could not possibly have happened—and did." More than that, she was a social force of some importance because she galvanized a then-comatose movement, Feminism, into an activity that has never ceased. Finally she, like Phryne, was just too beautiful to be hanged. In the rout of odd characters that compose the Lunatic Fringe of American reform movements she is the one that charms the unregenerate most of all, partly because of her incredibility, but largely because of her complete humanity.

Old Buck was a bum and Roxy, his wife, was a slut. By all rules of eugenics this unappetizing pair should have produced offspring revolting in appearance and deplorable in their moral and mental traits; instead of which they engendered five children, all of whom were endowed with physical beauty and two of whom were touched with genius. So from the very beginning the story is all wrong. "Everything's got a moral," said the Duchess, "if only you can find it." But this story, having no moral, flatly contradicts the Duchess; so to the extent that the manners and customs of Americans belong to *Alice in Wonderland,* this story is heretical and subversive, therefore should be forgotten.

But it so happens that some Americans are not Lewis Carroll characters. Some believe in looking facts in the face. They are, perhaps, subversive characters, but somehow history has a way of justifying them in the long run. These face the fact that Buck and Roxy produced handsome children, two of them intelligent, highly so; and if the whole theory of eugenics collapses before that brutal fact, so much the worse for the theory of eugenics.

The origin of Reuben Buckman Claflin is shrouded in obscurity.* There was a Governor Claflin of Massachusetts (1869 to 1871) who derived the name from one Robert Mackclothlan, or Mackclaflin, a Scot who was a townsman of Wenham, Massachusetts, in 1661. Possibly Buck Claflin was descended from the same family, but if so his ancestor must have been some son of the Mackclothlan clan who wandered off—possibly because the police showed an embarrassing interest in his activities—and was conveniently forgotten by the respectable members of the tribe.

Be that as it may, this story starts with Buck for the sufficient reason that we know nothing of his ancestry. Buck married Roxanna Hummel and she, too, is definitely the beginning of her line. All we can say of Roxanna is all we can

* A friendly genealogist contends that this is all wrong. He claims to have traced Buck's ancestry directly to Robert Mackclothlan (or Mackclaflin) who was undoubtedly an ancestor of William Claflin, Governor of Massachusetts, 1869 to 1871. My genealogist also asserts flatly that the name is a corruption of the well-known Scottish name, MacLaughlin. As it happens, the writer is acquainted with a number of the MacLaughlins, who are such eminently respectable people that he declines to be associated with any attempt to impose Buck upon them. He merely reports the charge, leaving it to the MacLaughlins to take care of themselves.

say of Eve, namely, that she represents the female of the species. Whence she came is lost in the mists of oblivion, which is perhaps just as well, since there is nothing in her history to suggest that her genealogy would be edifying.

Both were philoprogenitive which, if it be a virtue, is about the only virtue that can be ascribed to either. Buck was worthless, and Roxy was worthless in spades. That, in a sentence, is the history of the Claflin family in the first generation. But Buck had a certain low cunning that commands no admiration, yet did have a definite survival value; and Roxy was just too mean to die. So they lived into old age, preying upon their offspring and through them upon society.

It is remarkable that out of the litter of juvenile delinquents produced by this disagreeable pair only three became anything like social menaces. Five of the ten children apparently did not survive to maturity, and of the other five two girls made marriages that were not too bad by any standard and that by the Claflin standard were remarkably successful. One was so nearly normal that she may be dismissed as playing no relevant part in this story. The other, handicapped from the start by the daunting name of Utica, lived a fairly conventional life for a good many years; but when her sisters acquired national notoriety she seems to have been consumed by envy. It drove her to malicious attacks upon them, and when that failed to gain her anything but widespread contempt, she took to the bottle and eventually drank herself to death.

The one male in the group, named Hebern, had the physical beauty and apparently something of the charm of his sisters. He posed as a cancer doctor, and while he was obviously a charlatan his activities had no perceptable effect upon history. Indeed, in those years the most conscientious doctors in the world knew so little about treatment of cancer that Hebern's therapy may not have been perceptibly worse than any other. No doubt he speeded the exit from this vale of tears of many victims of the malady, but that he killed them any faster than the most reputable practitioners is open to doubt. He contributed nothing to our knowledge of cancer, but neither did he subtract anything. He was a nullity and may be dismissed from consideration.

The marvels of the age were the seventh and ninth children named, respectively, Victoria and Tennessee; and of these Victoria was the really dynamic force, although for a long time Tennessee overshadowed her in notoriety. Tennessee seems to have been merely a great courtesan, but Victoria had some of the elements of a great woman, among them being a masterful ability to turn Tennessee's sex appeal to more than a pecuniary profit. Through it, and her own, they acquired not only cash but influence, followers and a certain measure of dignity. Between them they constituted a social force of immense potency and unquestionably affected the history of the United States appreciably.

Time favored them. Victoria was born in 1838, Tennessee in 1846, so at the end of the Civil War they were twenty-seven and nineteen years old respectively. The ten years following that war were what Claude G. Bowers called "The Tragic Era," on account of the blatancy of its chicanery and fraud. The prevalence of rascals may have been no greater, statistically, then than at other periods, but they were more prominent and very much gaudier than ever before or since.

But "tragic" is a questionable adjective to apply to an era with such a broadly comic aspect. Not only its villainies, but its most pretentious moralities had a farcical element that makes any candid history of those years as uproarious as it is astounding. "Uncle Dan" Drew, Jim Fiske, Jay Gould and Commodore Vanderbilt were among the business tycoons of the time and, if their battles were murderous, they were also humorous—with a rather bawdy humor, no doubt, but fetching all the same. Great millionaires skipping over ditches and fences just one jump ahead of the sheriff presented a marvelous spectacle to the rejoicing galleries, even though it was one whose social implications were grim enough.

Yet the absurdities of the business world were as nothing compared to those of the moral and religious leadership of the period. Puritanism was then in the last stages of decay. The profound moral earnestness that had made it great in its best days had largely evaporated, leaving little but the hollow shell of superstition and hypocrisy with which it had become incrusted. John Calvin had been replaced by Tartuffe.

Of course this was not absolute. There were living from 1865 to 1875 some of the wisest and noblest men and women that have graced American history at any time, and they were the saving forces that eventually pulled the country out of the slough. But roughly speaking, the decade was one in which religion had degenerated into payment of tithes of anise and cummin and morality had become the art of not getting caught.

It was an environment singularly favorable to the flourishing of such a group as the Claflin tribe. Their first clear appearance in history was in the country village of Homer, some thirty miles northeast of Columbus, Ohio, where they were the scandal of the community. Buck was not unsuccessful financially; he was a crafty trader, but he prospered more by skinning the other party to a deal than by an honest exchange of values and, as usually happens to shifty characters, he gradually went downhill because fewer and fewer people would risk doing business with him.

Roxy was a slatternly housewife and her method of discipline consisted of alternately screaming at the children and slobbering over them. Naturally, they were wild, unkempt and, as they grew older, neighborhood terrors. Eventually they were completely ostracized; self-respecting mothers forbade their children to set foot on the Claflin premises and would not allow the Claflins to come on their own property.

Things came to a head when Buck, having somehow acquired title to a local gristmill, insured it heavily and the mill promptly burned. Buck had an alibi of sorts, but it was pretty shaky—he had ostensibly gone to a neighboring town that day, but he was reported as seen halfway back shortly after dark and an hour or two before the fire was discovered. In any event, the village was not much interested in "nice, sharp quillets of the law." A citizens' committee called on Buck; and while he might have had an alibi, it was certain that they had plenty of determination and plenty of rope. Under the circumstances, Buck chose not to argue the point; he disappeared between two days.

That left the family stranded and Roxy and her brood were not exactly God's gift to any community. Yet Homer, while it could be heavy-handed, was not devoid of social conscience. After various expedients had been tried the people held what was called a "benefit" to which everybody contributed, and through it they raised money enough to get the Claflins out of town.

Exactly where they went is still unknown, but they met Buck somewhere and presently they began to appear in various Ohio towns, operating as spiritualists and mesmerists, Victoria and Tennessee being the star performers. In this set-up Tennessee, ever the hard-boiled opportunist, was probably completely cynical, but there is evidence that Victoria was not. As a child—she said from the age of three—she had been subject to fits of a kind of self-hypnosis, during which she claimed to be subject to a spirit control. After some years she identified this control as Demosthenes, the Greek orator, and there is little doubt that at some times, in some circumstances, she half-believed in the reality of this power. It is significant that her control was a man of eloquence.

The terrific emotional stresses of a great war always create golden opportunities for persons who claim contact with another world, and invariably quacks of every variety flourish. For some years the Claflins did well. The chances are that they could have done fabulously well if there had been any real cohesion within the group. Buck took over the business management. Hebern, the son, dispensed his cancer cures. Victoria and Tennessee went into trances and communicated with the dead; they also practiced healing by mesmerism and the laying on of hands. Roxy was responsible for cooking up vast quantities of a nostrum called an elixir and sold in bottles with Tennessee's picture on the label. It was a medicine show of vast potentialities, only briefly embarrassed when Tennessee was indicted for manslaughter after one of her cancer patients died somewhat too rapidly, and the family had to do a precipitate fade-out.

But the organization had a fatal defect—the Claflins could not be satisfied with operating on the rubes, they must needs work on each other. Nobody was satisfied with his share of the take. Everybody wanted to boss the show. Two of the girls married and dropped out. Before she was sixteen Victoria also married a young doctor named Canning Woodhull, but instead of dropping out she attached her husband to the gang. Tennessee married, too, but not seriously. She changed her name indeed, but not to Bartels, that of her husband; by this time that name on the elixir bottles was too good a commercial property to abandon; she merely began to sign it "Tennie C. Claflin," and Bartels remained a shadowy figure soon to fade away completely. Victoria, however, not only called herself Woodhull, but bore two children to the doctor, one of whom, a daughter with the alluring name of Zulu Maud, survived her.

Victoria's dissatisfaction with the Claflin circus was based on something more than avarice. She resented being exploited by her family, but beyond that she disliked the medicine show itself; she burned to do something more important than swindling country bumpkins and she felt within her the power to play a far more impressive part on a vastly larger stage. Eventually she persuaded Tennessee to drop the nostrum-peddling and to join her in setting up as spiritualists on their own. This thrust Buck, Roxy and Hebern into the background, which they did not like, and they showed their resentment by creating all the trouble they could. Nevertheless it was a sagacious move, for the sisters were superbly equipped for a career in the shadowy realm that lies between complete probity and outright crime.

Tennessee was the simpler and more obvious character. Bewitchingly pretty, she had picked up somewhere in the course of her dubious career the superficial aspect of a *grande dame*. Sex was her stock in trade, but she was far indeed from being a woman of the streets. She had mastered the art of pleasing men not by gross carnality, but by a subtle approach that could convince even a man of intelligence that he had been singled out by a charming woman for favors that ordinary brutes could not attain, or appreciate if they had attained them. To men of sense flattery is potent in measure as it is delicately applied, and Tennessee's application could be as feathery light and yet as sure as the touch of her hands in her mesmeric massage. So, repeatedly, persons who were most certainly men of sense testified fervently to the grace, dignity and obvious good breeding of this lady. Not until they were hopelessly involved and she began to turn the screw to bleed them financially did they change their opinion, and not always even then.

But Victoria was a far more remarkable phenomenon than her sister. To begin with, she had everything that Tennessee had, physically. Indeed, the testimony is unanimous that where Tennessee was pretty, Victoria was really beautiful. Then to her physical perfection she added a quickness of comprehension that was a workable substitute for intelligence. There is no indication that she ever had an original idea in her life, but if an original idea was presented she could grasp the essential point with astonishing speed. So men who had ideas found it delightful to talk with her and usually rated her intellectual ability well above its actual value.

Victoria's success was not confined to men. A woman endowed with all it takes to make a really great courtesan is usually hated by women, and so it was with the Claflin sisters. Their worst defeats were administered by women. But the feminine intellectuals were less hostile, especially those fanatically devoted to a cause that the Claflins might help. So it came about that Susan B. Anthony and Elizabeth Cady Stanton, the suffrage leaders, delighted in Victoria. True, Julia Ward Howe and Mary Rice Livermore, leaders of the more conservative feminists, would have none of her, but they were always more interested in morals than in Women's Rights.

It was in 1868 that this pair moved upon New York and began the ten years that were to emblazon them indelibly upon American history. In the meantime their domestic arrangements had reached an unbelievable degree of complication. Tennessee's husband had faded out of the picture, but Victoria's had not. Later, one of his successors in Victoria's affections was to describe Canning Woodhull as a monster, but apparently he was only a dismal sort of weakling, incapable of managing or even holding the human dynamo he had married. Somewhere along the line Victoria simply dismissed him and transferred her affections to one James Blood, a considerably more virile specimen and a man of some intellectual power. Eventually Victoria divorced Woodhull and is supposed to have married Blood in 1866; one of her biographers, Beril Becker, is convinced that this was the great love of her life, but the other, Emanie Sachs, is more skeptical. Nobody doubts, though, that Blood served her splendidly as a ghost writer.

But the discarded Woodhull hit the downgrade for skid row. He became a drug addict and a human derelict, incapable of taking care of himself; whereupon Victoria took him back into her household, although not as a husband. Naturally, the regime caused comment, and it was undoubtedly the sting of the comment that turned her mind more and more to the invidious position to which women were relegated by the manners and customs of the times.

Victoria was not in the least a philosophical Feminist. She had neither the intellectual nor the social background to formulate a program on abstract principles. She was a Feminist not because the position of women in 1868 was unjust and disabling to half the human race but because it was unjust and disabling to a specific individual, to wit, Victoria Woodhull. But for the very reason that she was pleading her own case her attack was direct and driven home with tremendous emotional power.

"Her oratory was paroxysmal," says Sachs, "jammed with such passionate impulses to proclaim that when she released them she jerked people out of the everyday world."

Nobody arguing an abstraction ever did that. It is when the orator is himself a victim of the conditions he assails, and his words are imbued with the bitterness of personal experience, that he approaches domination of the emotions of his audience. It was her passionate resentment of injustices perpetrated upon her that made this woman a genuine firebrand. Blood was an able assistant who could supply her with smoothly turned phrases to which her emotional intensity lent a tremendous impact; and shortly after her arrival in New York she picked up another henchman equally useful.

This was Stephen Pearl Andrews, himself an oddity worthy to be bracketed with Woodhull or any other eccentric. Andrews was of the intellectual aristocracy. His family had been known in Massachusetts since 1643 and for generations had been producing clergymen and writers of distinction. They were nonconformists of the Roger Williams type. Stephen's father, the Reverend Elisha Andrews, was a theological disputant counted among the most distinguished of Baptist scholars; but the family culminated in Stephen's nephew, Elisha Benjamin Andrews, the famous "Bennie," president of Brown University, and credited with bringing that institution into the forefront of modern centers of higher learning.

Stephen's intellectual capacity rivaled that of the best of the Andrews tribe, but he lacked the balance that made the others powerful. He was an astounding linguist. It was said that he knew thirty-two languages, and he invented a thirty-third, called Alwato, a forerunner of Esperanto and other universal languages. At the age of nineteen he went to New Orleans, studied law, married a Southern girl and became a thundering abolitionist. Removing to Houston, Texas, he became a leader of the bar, but ruined his prospects by his violent opposition to slavery. In 1843 he was mobbed and driven out of the town, whereupon he went to England and tried to interest the British government in a scheme for emancipation by purchase of the slaves. He failed in that, but he encountered the Pitman system of writing shorthand and introduced it into America, establishing a school of phonography that is to say, shorthand, in Boston five years before Benn Pitman appeared in Cincinnati.

In 1847 he removed to New York and imitated Sir Francis Bacon by undertaking a compendium of universal science. His social system, which he called "Pantarchy," included odds and ends of every radical idea that was floating around. The rights of women had a prominent place in it and he included in those rights sexual freedom. This interested Victoria Woodhull and she sought out Stephen Pearl Andrews, whom she charmed as effectually as she did most men. Soon he was putting his skill at her service.

Now Victoria was equipped to go to town in a really big way. With Blood to give her utterances a smooth and flowing style, with Andrews to touch them with quite genuine learning, and with her own personal charm, she could speak and write with great effectiveness. More than that, she had an audience, for between them she and Tennessee had achieved a notoriety that forced them upon the notice of every resident of New York. Among those curious enough to look them up was Cornelius Vanderbilt, known as the Commodore, the tough and powerful founder of the Vanderbilt fortune.

In 1868 the Commodore was seventy-four years old and he was thinking much oftener of the other world than he had thought in his twenties when he was lustily battling the Fulton-Livingston crowd for the ferryboat business in New York, or even in his sixties when he was smashing the filibuster William Walker in Central America. So when this new pair of occultists appeared in the city it was inevitable that he should be interested; and when he met them he was as completely charmed as other men and, to a certain extent, was conquered.

But Vanderbilt even in his old age was of much tougher fiber than the men whom the Claflins enslaved. He enjoyed their society and admitted it. He gladly loaded them with favors. Apparently there was a moment when he seriously considered marrying Tennessee, and he constantly demanded her services as a mesmeric masseuse; but the sisters never took the old boy completely into camp.

He made them rich in a spectacular way. Victoria had long contended that if the American woman remained in a state of tutelage it was largely her own fault, because she was too spiritless to fight for her rights. There was the field of business, for instance. Only convention, not legal barriers, said Victoria, prevented women from entering it. So she and Tennessee did. They set up the brokerage house of Woodhull & Claflin in Wall Street. Old Vanderbilt, hugely amused, probably furnished some of the capital, and certainly gave them valuable tips by which they cleaned up handsomely in the stock market.

The furore created by this crashing frontal assault on the prevailing mores is beyond description, especially as the unregenerate caste of newspaper reporters found it an inexhaustible source of amusing stories. Then Victoria seized every opportunity to inflame the stodgily conventional by increasing activity in public life. She became a popular lecturer on Women's Rights.

The usual concept of a feminist at the time was that of a mannish creature with the build of a stevedore and the voice of a foghorn, a caricature of womanhood revolting to every male instinct. So when the crowds saw appear on the platform an exquisite and apparently fragile figure, feminine to the finger tips, the effect was a titillating shock. Add, then, an address couched in Blood's suave and supple prose, and studded with arguments historical, anthropological, economic and philosophical drawn from Andrews' enormous store of learning and the effect was redoubled. She was a smash hit.

Yet there was another element supplied by nobody but the

woman herself, and it probably had more to do with the effect she produced than all the rest combined. This was a moral courage that did not blench before any implication of her doctrine. It was conspicuously a mealymouthed generation and Victoria Woodhull was not mealymouthed. If they charged her with advocating free love she met the charge head-on with an assertion that no adultery could be as foul as for a woman to maintain marital relations with a man she loathed, and if she happened to be married to him that made it all the more foul, for in that case society itself participated in the villainy.

About the year 1870 this was terrific, but it had an effect that the conventional did not expect and could not account for. It gave the impression of a fundamental honesty that all Victoria's scarlet sins could not eradicate. Even the scandalized felt that on this subject if no other, Victoria Woodhull was telling the truth as she saw it and telling it with superb courage.

As for the enthusiasts, they went wild. Elizabeth Cady Stanton, for example, wrote, "The nature that can pass through all phases of social degradation, vice, crime, poverty and temptation in all its forms, and yet maintain a dignity and purity of character through all, gives unmistakable proof of its high origin, its divinity." Mrs. Stanton was more impassioned than exact. Ascribing divinity to Victoria is pretty strong, even for the modern taste; but the passage does demonstrate the impact of this personality upon an unusually strong intelligence.

The platform, however, soon became an inadequate medium for Victoria. In 1870 the sisters began publication of *Woodhull and Claflin's Weekly,* one of the most curious ventures in the history of American journalism, filled though that history is with fantastic incidents. The *Weekly* defies classification because there is hardly an adjective in the language applicable to any newspaper that does not apply to this one. Sachs covered part of it with the remark that, "like Victoria herself, it was silly and venomous and sublime."

Its primary purpose, announced in the first issue, was to support Victoria Claflin Woodhull for President of the United States. But aside from that there was hardly a measure of social amelioration that it did not advocate brilliantly, and hardly a depth of depravity that it failed to touch. Blood and Andrews did the bulk of the writing, but they had effective assistance from other contributors, some of them exceedingly able people, others as crazy as anything outside of Bedlam. Feminism was the *Weekly's* dominant interest, but it assailed entrenched injustice in many forms. There was scarcely an issue in which it did not peel the paint off some whited sepulchre, often with great journalistic and literary skill; on the other hand, there was scarcely an issue in which it did not back some charlatanry that might have made Cagliostro blush. It argued the cause of labor with eloquence and skill; it presented some astonishingly acute judgments on economic and fiscal policy; it collected an honorable array of enemies among venal and corrupt politicians. But intermixed with this excellent and socially valuable journalism it ran articles publicizing some of the most outrageous quacks in the country, especially those pretending to deal with the occult.

The *Weekly* had an even darker side. As Victoria's public life became busier, so Tennessee's private—very private—life grew more active. Naturally there are no records, so exact information on the subject is nonexistent; but that Tennessee used the *Weekly* to put the bite on the boy friends seems established beyond a reasonable doubt. Toward the end she published a letter signed with an obviously assumed name, but purporting to come from the madam of the fanciest brothel in New York. The writer said she was retiring from business and on the eve of going abroad she was delivering to the *Weekly* ledgers in which she had recorded the correct name and address of her customers for the past twenty years. It was a fraud. Tennessee wrote the letter herself; but there was probably some ground for the contemporary opinion that it brought into the coffers of the *Weekly* a flood of money from prosperous and dignified citizens who preferred to take no chances on the publication of any such records.

The fury that such activities built up against the enterprising sisters was boundless, but for a long time it was impotent. Their magnetic charm rendered them invulnerable, and their shrewdness reached higher and higher. Victoria snared one of the most eminent journalists in America, Theodore Tilton, editor of the *Independent*, a quasi-religious journal of opinion with immense influence, and for six months, by her own account, the affair was torrid.

There is no convincing evidence that this was a simulated passion. Tilton had more than a good mind and an influential position; all witnesses agree that he was a charming fellow, and it is probable that when Victoria first fell in love with him she had no ulterior purpose in mind. He was married, but her philosophy of free love made that no obstacle. True, this philosophy was not proof against emotion; once when she caught Jim Blood with his arms around another woman she threw a pair of shears at them. Freedom didn't extend to Jim.

But the connection with Tilton brought Victoria to the great crisis of her career and betrayed her into the error of assailing the one invulnerable citadel in America, namely, piety. It was not religion. There is only too much evidence to support the belief that in 1872 genuine religion in the United States was almost at its lowest ebb; but the country's piety, that is, its acceptance of the forms of religion, was colossal and impregnable.

It was so great that churches had come to be profitable commercial investments, much as movie houses were fifty years later. It was nothing uncommon for a wealthy real-estate operator to sink many thousands in a church building and to spend other thousands hiring the most popular preacher available to preach there. The real-estate man would then promote the organization of a congregation that would pay rent for the building, or purchase it at a handsome profit, the money coming partly from special gifts, but largely from the Sunday collections. As a rule these entrepreneurs were extremely broad-minded about the brand of religion propagated in their churches. They demanded that it be of a kind that would charm the shekels from the congregational pockets, but beyond that they were tolerant to a high degree.

The result was the rise of a profession not exactly matched by anything in existence today. The nearest parallel, perhaps, is the radio or television commentator, whose first job is to be interesting. If he can at the same time be truthful and intelligent, so much the better, but he *must* be interesting, or he is quickly off the air.

The popular preacher of 1872 was under the same necessity, but he had another commitment from which the commentator is free. He had to establish some relation, however tenuous, between his discourse and religion. Frequently that relation was tenuous indeed; the preacher might devote fifty-five minutes out of the hour to politics, sociology, economics or whatever topic might be engaging public attention at the moment, but if he put in five minutes on religion his sermon was regarded as satisfactory.

In 1872 the most eminent member of this profession was the Reverend Dr. Henry Ward Beecher, preaching at Plymouth Church, in Brooklyn, an enormously expensive real-estate venture that was paying off handsomely. Beecher was a member of a family as much in the public eye then as the Eisenhowers and the Roosevelts are today. His father, the

Reverend Dr. Lyman Beecher, had been a formidable theologian and an even more formidable political force. Two brothers, Charles and Edward, were preachers of eminence and prolific writers. One sister, Catharine, was the most violent anti-suffragist of her day and at the same time such a powerful advocate of female education that she had strewn women's colleges throughout the South and West. Another sister, Harriet Beecher Stowe, had written *Uncle Tom's Cabin*, the book that Lincoln, not altogether facetiously, credited with precipitating the Civil War.

But in 1872 Henry Ward Beecher was outshining them all. He was, in the slang of a later day, "some hunk of a man," sturdy, full-blooded, tremendously vital. As a theologian he was not impressive, but as an exhorter he had few equals and no superior on the continent. Like Macklin, the actor, Beecher could recite the multiplication table and charge it with an emotional pressure that "drew iron tears down Pluto's cheek."

He was, needless to say, an immensely valuable property to the financial backers of his church. He was also a hypocrite in the eyes of some and a holy martyr in the eyes of others. In 1872 no third evaluation was deemed possible, but we have learned much about how the emotions operate and in the light of the knowledge gained since Beecher's day a judgment less extreme is possible. We know that mysticism and eroticism are so close together that an emotion originally stimulated by one may easily carry over into the other without conscious intent. The sermons of Henry Ward Beecher were intensely emotional, and if that emotion occasionally became more carnal than spiritual, it was to be expected and is no proof that the man deliberately planned any deception.

The Tiltons, warm supporters of Beecher, were also emotionally intense and presently the preacher was involved with Tilton's wife. He said that their intimacy stopped short of carnal knowledge; she said that it didn't; but all parties agree that Mrs. Tilton made a confession to her husband and an unsavory mess developed. There was a conference among the three that resulted in the drawing up and signing of a weird document in which Tilton virtually condoned his wife's misconduct and Beecher, without explicitly admitting that it had happened, promised that it should never happen again.

A thing like that can seldom be hushed up under any circumstances, and when the three people involved are all emotionally unstable it is flatly impossible. The facts soon came to be known to an increasing number of people, Victoria Woodhull among them. Her interest at first was perfunctory. She was on friendly terms with Beecher and he had done no more than apply her doctrine of free love. She had no interest either in exposing the affair, or in covering it up.

The people most desperately anxious to hide it were those with a direct interest in the continuing prosperity of Plymouth Church, some because their money, others because their prestige was at stake. But they were joined by large numbers of the pious with no particular interest in Plymouth Church but apparently committed to the view that morality and religion have no inner strength of their own, but stand or fall with their human protagonists. These contended that even if the story were true it must be suppressed because religion and morality would be discredited with the discrediting of the Reverend Henry Ward Beecher. If the charge of hypocrisy is to be brought against anybody it should be these people rather than Beecher.

The thing had been stewing under cover for a year or more and the lid might have been kept on longer had Beecher had no sisters. But he had, and they were strong-minded women. In 1872 Harriet and Catharine made up their minds that it

was up to them to run the Claflin women out of New York.
Even so, there might have been no explosion had the Beecher
women been willing to stage a fair fight, for the woman never
lived whom the Claflins dared not meet in a battle that was
open and aboveboard.

But the Beechers didn't fight fairly. Instead, they brought
organized pressure to bear on one landlord after another to
evict the Claflins from their premises. Eventually they even
turned the heat on the keepers of public hotels, promising
to make trouble, not for the Claflins, but for anybody who
treated them decently.

Then Victoria lost her temper and in some measure her
judgment. She decided to teach the Beechers that two could
play at that game, and therefore issued an ultimatum to their
reverend brother. He would either call off his sisters—preferably by standing up for Victoria publicly—or she would let
him have it with both barrels, and she wasn't fooling.

It was bitterly unfair. Henry Ward Beecher may have been
a power in the pulpit, but in private life he was basically an
abject creature, and Harriet and Catharine were battle-axes.
He had no more chance of controlling them than Mr. Caspar
Milquetoast would have of taming a pair of Numidian lions,
and Victoria should have known it; but rage probably
blinded her to reality.

So in its issue of November 2, 1872, the *Weekly* broke
wide open the whole story of the Beecher-Tilton connection.

Its effect was like a rainmaker's "seeding" the clouds. It
instantly precipitated every vaporous lunacy floating in the
intellectual atmosphere and the deluge was beyond belief.
The first insanity was perpetrated by the supporters of
Beecher, morals and religion. They clapped the Claflins in
jail on the charge of issuing an obscene publication. This
was nonsense, for the story was not obscene, it was merely
libelous—provided Beecher could prove it untrue. The Claf-

lins were soon released, but their arrest brought into action on opposite sides two of the most fantastic figures in American history, Anthony Comstock and George Francis Train.

Comstock was anti-Claflin and his activity in this case gave him the start on his long career of harrying and harassing in the name of purity every writer or artist who presented to the American public an original idea. Train was pro-Claflin, an eccentric genius who had been growing more erratic every year, and who seems to have been completely knocked loose from his moorings by the Claflin affair.

He had made a great deal of money, first as a shipping magnate—it was his firm that commissioned Donald McKay to build the *Flying Cloud,* greatest of clipper ships—and later as a traction magnate, in England, in Australia and in various states of the Union. Becoming affluent, he abandoned business and apparently set out to amuse himself; he became a Fenian to bedevil the British, and in 1870 a communist to bedevil the French; he read Jules Verne and promptly went around the world in eighty days; he built a villa in Newport; and for the three years following 1869 continually made speeches advocating himself for President.

Naturally, the Claflin affair enthralled him. He too had a paper, called the *Train Ligne,* in which he defended the sisters. He published choice excerpts culled from the Bible to show the authorities that the Tilton-Beecher article was far less obscene than Holy Writ; so in their frenzy they jugged Train, too. He refused to put up bail or pay a fine, and when they released him at last he appeared on the streets of New York holding an umbrella over his head but stark naked.

Volumes would be required to record all the ravings that followed the breaking open of the scandal, for the country really was set by the ears when piety received a body blow. But piety rallied and grimly set about the business of exterminating the disturbers of its peace. This proved difficult, but it was pursued relentlessly. Beecher, well advised by hardheaded lawyers, refused to sue the Claflins, and eventually Tilton sued him. The case resulted in a hung jury. Nine of the jurors were for Beecher, or at least against Tilton, but three believed the charges, and at least one-fourth of the public joined the three. Beecher continued to preach for a dozen years, but never again was his voice accepted as thunder from Sinai.

His friends, however—greatly assisted by other members of the Claflin family—closed in on Victoria and Tennessee, and by 1877, two years after the Beecher trial, it appeared to be only a matter of time until they would be crushed completely. Then the old Commodore died and it is commonly believed that his death gave them their final triumph over their foes. It came about through the peculiar provisions of his will. His slight esteem for his son Cornelius was evidenced by the fact that he left him $200,000; his opinion of women in general is evidenced by the fact that he left each of his daughters $500,000; while to his son William, who had shown real business capacity, went the residue of the estate, about $90,000,000. The other children tried to break the will, and when it appeared that the case was about to come to trial, someone, probably a shrewd lawyer, had the dreadful thought that the contestants might call the Claflins as witnesses to prove the old man's incompetence.

Even though he had withdrawn his public support the Commodore had always liked them and had continued to see them almost to the end of his days. So, although they were not mentioned in the will and were not parties to the suit, it was highly probable that the court would admit their testimony; and the very thought of what those women might say on the witness stand was enough to give any trial lawyer palpitations of the heart.

Eliminating them was the most obvious of precautions.

What was done about it nobody knows, for it was done most discreetly. All that is certain is that the Claflins, who had appeared to be in dire financial straits, suddenly left for England with money in their purses and the will case was settled out of court. Gossip asserted that it took half a million to move them; and under the circumstances it was probably well worth it.

Notoriety followed them abroad, of course, but in England it was merely the notoriety attaching to radical advocates of Women's Rights. This closed certain doors to them, but it opened others. The more squalid episodes in their history seem never to have been widely known in London, or if they were the Claflin charm was able to overcome them. The gossip was not able to prevent Victoria's marriage to a rich and prominent banker or Tennessee's to an English baronet, later to be a Portuguese marquis.

"Everything's got a moral if you can only find it," said the Duchess, and of course the Claflin story has a very obvious moral, but it just won't do. The obvious moral is that crime does pay, and in the American scheme of things that is unconstitutional, so the story has been carefully forgotten by all true believers in the Uplift. Nevertheless, it is there. Like Joan of Arc, it couldn't possibly have happened—but did. An apparently worthless woman jarred this nation right down to its heels and laid prostrate a number of swelling reputations and a larger number of swollen conventions and punctilios; and this inevitably raises the question, was she in fact worthless?

After all, Victoria Woodhull never championed adultery, swindling and blackmail, however much she may have practiced them. The things she advocated were, practically without exception, things that later generations have accepted as worthy ideals. The right of a woman to be accepted on her merits as a human being without reference to gender is no longer questioned. Even sincere opponents of easy divorce admit that a loveless marriage is a source of innumerable evils. The dignity of the individual, including the female individual, is now called the fundamental principle of our way of life.

Victoria Woodhull spoke up for all these things when it was dangerous to do so. That is to say, she spoke the truth courageously, and no man or woman has ever yet defied peril to speak truth without producing a profound and lasting effect.

Grant that her story is the most uproarious farce that the Lunatic Fringe has produced, it cannot be denied that the episode gave to the then lethargic cause of Women's Rights a dynamic—or, if you prefer, a demonic—drive that it has never completely lost.

These were triumphs of no trifling magnitude; and if Victoria achieved her victories somewhat after the fashion of the haetera Phryne, nevertheless she triumphed.

7

proem

Slavery, that cannibalistic fallacy that swallowed up almost every other line of thinking in the United States from the day of the Virginia Dynasty to that of Appomattox, was finally destroyed in 1865. But the power of abstract thinking, and especially the art of constructing sound hypotheses, was slow to revive. Not for a dozen years after the end of the war was a brilliantly original thesis devised in America, and then it came from an unexpected quarter and was based upon a theme that Jefferson and John Adams hardly touched.

In the meantime the substance of power had shifted from the hands of political theorists into those of the economic overlords. In the year 1877 politicians still held the offices, but business men held the strings to which they danced. The common man's problem was no longer to prove that his right to freedom could be traced back to the Anglo-Saxon witenagemot, but how to exercise that freedom without depriving himself of bread.

This problem was more and more engaging the attention of the pundits in the universities, but it also engaged that of a printer in California; and he brought to it a freshness of mind and an intellectual daring sadly lacking in the schools. Naturally he was regarded as a lunatic; but he jarred the structure of economic and political thought. He was consigned to oblivion for a while, but by strange ways and by strange hands his work has been revived in recent years and his stature steadily increases.

Read, then, the tale of:

HENRY GEORGE

who hated the bitch goddess

IN THE FIFTIES of the twentieth century Henry George rose from the dead in truly spectacular fashion. In 1897 they buried his ideas with his body, and for fifty years he remained little more than one of what Jefferson called "monuments of the safety with which error of opinion may be tolerated where reason is left free to combat it." Jefferson indeed would have objected to the application of his words to George, for he was thinking of a different type; but the description corresponds to the view of this man generally held for half a century.

The resurrection is attributable in part to a pair of biographies published, one in 1950, the other in 1955, both notable books, although for different reasons.* One was the work of George's daughter, the other an evaluation by a professional historian not affected by any personal relation to his subject.

Filial piety was admittedly the inspiration of Mrs. de Mille's book, so as regards George's philosophy and influence in the world it carries no great weight of authority; but it is unusual in its presentation of a personality of extraordinary sweetness and charm. Henry George was not what is colloquially described as "a good provider"; on the contrary, he

* *Henry George: Citizen of the World,* by Anna George de Mille, 1950. *Henry George,* by Charles Albro Barker, 1955.

was a lamentably poor one as genius frequently is. But he won and held the adoration of his family, which is by no means characteristic of genius. The book therefore is authoritative in demonstrating the fundamental integrity that affected everything the man did.

Dr. Barker, on the other hand, approached his subject unemotionally, unless it is emotional to cherish a high admiration for an extraordinary mind. His judgments are cool, temperate and based always on the record, not on personal impressions; yet to a considerable extent, indeed to an astonishing extent, he supports what one would naturally assume are the more impulsive findings of the daughter. Together they leave the unbiased reader no room to doubt that Henry George's ideas are still influencing the trend of thought, which is to say, he is no tombstone but a dynamic force, intellectually very much alive.

Yet the books, of course, are but signal flags, responsible for our awareness of George, but not for his resurgence. A dead author who rises from the tomb always comes up under his own power, and always for the same reason, namely, that a later generation discovers that his ideas correspond to reality much more closely than had been supposed. It is not necessarily the reality of his own time; he may have been wide of the mark while he lived and therefore of little use to his contemporaries; yet the meanderings of the stream of history may bring him in line with the main currents of thought a decade, or a generation, or a century after he has departed this life. This seems to be the case of Henry George. Some of what he said—not all, by any means—has been much more useful to our generation when it was repeated by Keynes, or Laski, or Roosevelt, or Tugwell than it was when it was first enunciated by George himself.

This is not an insinuation that the moderns are low fellows addicted to plagiarism. If they have frequently quoted

George without credit it is because they did not, and humanly speaking could not know to whom credit was due. When he was most original George was seldom able to express his idea in the sharply vivid phrase that clings to the memory, as David Harum said, "like a burr to a cow's tail." So his best thought was often expressed in terms only partially comprehensible to his contemporaries but that acquired meaning from subsequent events, when most people had forgotten that George said anything on the subject. Thus he merged into the background and was lost for years; and when he emerged it was less as an individual than as an influence on the climate of opinion, like those Arctic hurricanes that determine the weather in the United States although Americans are not aware that they ever blew.

As late as ten years ago almost everybody who remembered George at all remembered him as the great Single Taxer, which is much like remembering Sir William Osler as the man who favored chloroforming people at forty, and Sir Isaac Newton as one who amused himself by watching apples fall. Henry George did advocate the single tax, but only as one of many expedients directed to the goal of equality of opportunity, and toward the end of his life he was annoyed by people's tendency to sum up his whole philosophy in this one expedient.

His career was remarkably variegated, yet remarkably humdrum. The latter statement may seem to be a contradiction in terms, but it isn't. Henry George had the faculty of taking the color out of things in a really remarkable degree. Born in Philadelphia in 1839 he was one of eleven children of a minor official in the customs service. His father at one time had been in the business of publishing religious books without any great success, but without calamitous failure; he returned to a salaried job about the time of Henry's birth.

The original George, Henry's grandfather, was an English sea captain who made some money, which his children were unable to keep. Henry's father married a woman of Scottish descent; both were devout Episcopalians and Henry was brought up in that faith, adhering to it all his life although he was never conspicuously pious.

His formal schooling ended before he was fifteen, but what there was of it seems to have been good. After a year in various clerkships he went to sea and made voyages to India and Australia, ending in California, where he learned the printing trade and graduated from that into journalism. His observation of what went on during the California land boom led to the writing of his one really famous book, *Progress and Poverty*. In 1880 he removed to New York. His book had attracted a good deal of attention in Europe where he made many valuable contacts and became interested in the Irish land question on which he wrote at length, spending much time in Europe organizing various tax reform groups.

His disgust with the corruption of the Gilded Age, and especially with the Tammany regime in New York led in 1884 to his nomination for mayor on a reform ticket, against Abram S. Hewitt, Democrat, and Theodore Roosevelt, Republican. Hewitt won with 90,000 votes, against George's 68,000 and Roosevelt's 60,000—such, at least, were the official figures, although how many votes Tammany stole for Hewitt is anybody's guess. If the number ran as high as 12,000, then George was actually elected, as his more ardent supporters believed. At any rate he returned to writing and lecturing, spending more time in Great Britain and making one tour through Australia. In 1897 he was persuaded to run for mayor again, against his better judgment, and seemed to be making a very effective campaign when apoplexy struck him down and he died within a few hours, worn out at the age of fifty-eight.

As one studies the record, especially Barker's book, which is by far the most exact and detailed account, a curious and almost unbelievable pattern emerges. Again and again Henry George was not defeated by the machinations of his enemies, nor by his own mistakes, but simply recoiled from success. In his early days in the west he had a good start in the mercantile business in British Columbia, but as soon as things were going well he quit. In San Francisco when he got into journalism, he and a partner, after a terrible battle in which they teetered on the verge of bankruptcy a dozen times, got a real foothold with a newspaper that commanded much influence and seemed in a fair way to dominate the Pacific Coast; but as soon as the going became easy and large success was in plain sight, George withdrew. Twenty years later he was urged to settle in England and it is almost a certainty that he could have enjoyed ease and influence there; but he would not. It was almost as if he feared success—an oddity indeed, since he certainly feared nothing else; but perhaps like William James, he saw success as a bitch goddess and simply did not like her company.

The result was to make his story dull, depressing and definitely irritating. In addition to the instances cited, at one time or another he held a dozen excellent jobs which he sacrificed by quarreling—sometimes sedulously picking a quarrel—with the boss. But this is a familiar picture. Many men, including some of the most successful, are temperamentally incapable of working under the direction of others. The singularity of George is that he was apparently incapable of working under his own direction once it became clear that his work was going to succeed. In a jam he was wonderful—bold, tireless, resourceful and imperturbable—but as soon as the going became relatively easy all the drive seemed to go out of him, and he faltered and usually quit.

So the common practice of describing him as a frustrated

man is questionable. A man who is denied the fruits of his own labor is frustrated; but suppose he rejects them of his own volition—is he then to be called frustrated? Common sense may reply shortly that there are no such men; but in that case, let common sense undertake to explain Henry George and see how far it gets.

Perhaps at this point we are coming close to the factor that is the essence of the Lunatic Fringe. Success, after all, is deployed in depth, and even common sense admits that a man content with small achievements is a small man; the great one is he who makes his final objective the point of critical strategic importance and goes for it, indifferent to the success or failure of the preliminary skirmishing. Yet if a man has vision capable of locating the strategic point far beyond the horizon at an unattainable distance, common sense discards logic, and instead of calling him the greatest of all, calls him a lunatic.

What Henry George really wanted his generation did not know, our generation does not know, and if the man himself knew he was incapable of putting it into words. Obviously it was not money and ease; every man of first-rate ability likes distinction and so did he, but he never confused it with notoriety; it is clear that fame in the world was not the goal of his aspiration. The prodigious labor of all his days was to understand, but to what end? If we could answer that, we might be able to explain not this man only but also many another character that at present baffles historians. We might grasp the true inwardness of the Lunatic Fringe—and be overcome with astonishment.

The genesis of his *magnum opus* he recorded precisely. Having taken to the hills for a breath of air one day he looked down upon a California valley at the other side of which a new town was expanding. Fields stretching from the foot of the hill to the town were under cultivation, and George began to speculate on the destiny of the farmer. At the moment the value of his acres was measured by the value of the corn that his labor applied to the land would produce; but it was evident that in a few years the town would spread over the fields and then the land would be immensely more valuable, or at least would command an immensely greater price.

By what, then, would that price be measured? Obviously, by the presence of the townsmen, or by the values that the townsmen produced by their labor, not on the land, but in commerce and industry. Assuming that the farmer kept his land until this value had been created, he would grow rich, not by labor but by doing nothing. He would collect the value that the labor of others had created; and those who worked would remain poor. Progress, in short, was attended by poverty, and this struck Henry George as an absurdity.

The idea, of course, had occurred to a great many other people, including the German philosopher, Karl Marx. But it did not strike Marx as an absurdity; it struck him as a law of human existence, and he had already elaborated it in his immense treatise, *Das Kapital*. George could not have read Marx because when George wrote only one volume of Marx's work had been published and there was not yet an English translation; but when he did learn of the book years later he was not impressed. The concept of utter idiocy as a law of the universe was one that he could not entertain.

But if George did not know Marx, Marx knew George, all right, and his wrath against the American was Homeric. *Progress and Poverty* he damned as "an attempt, decked out with socialism, to save capitalist domination and indeed to establish it afresh on an even wider basis than its present one." Marx admitted that the man was "a talented writer" but with the furious addition that "he has also the repulsive presumption and arrogance which is displayed by all panacea

mongers without exception." Including, conspicuously, Karl
Marx.

It is true enough that *Progress and Poverty* contained a
glaring fallacy in its overestimation of the value of rent.
George assumed that if society appropriated rent the revenue
would be sufficient for the purpose of government without
the levying of any other tax, hence the phrase, "single tax,"
descriptive of his doctrine. A generation later it is plain that
this is a more than doubtful assumption. But it does not in-
validate the argument that the poverty attending progress
is the effect, not of immutable law, but of a defective, indeed,
an insensate economic organization.

The wrath of Marx is explained by the fact that this argument destroys the whole basis of communism. If the defects in a man-made economic system are the cause of our
woes, then it is reasonable to suppose that a better man-made
system might alleviate them. Only if one admits that men
are in the grip of impersonal historical forces that they can
neither oppose nor control does communist theory make
sense.

In this argument George was the somewhat cynical realist
and Marx the adherent of romantic mythology. Marx believed that capitalism, being the logical product of dialectical
materialism, was logically bound to crash from its own in-
herent weakness, and then the proletariat would come into
its own. George, believing that the defects of capitalism are
attributable to human folly and crime, saw no reason to
doubt that men, if they choose, can continue to be fools and
criminals indefinitely, therefore release of the proletariat
from oppression is by no means inevitable. If it is accomplished, it must be by their own efforts, and mainly by the
use of reason. To him communism was a form of escape

from reality, embraced by those too lazy or too stupid to cope with the world they live in.

Without doubt both men were products of their environment. Two and a half centuries of American history weighed relatively lightly upon George, especially as he didn't know much of it, by comparison with the fifty centuries of Old-World history that bore down upon Marx, especially as he knew all of it. But they both undertook to be prophets, dealing with the future; and in the cult of prophecy too much knowledge of failure and futility in the past may be a handicap rather than a help. Certainly the three-quarters of a century since they published (Marx in 1867, George in 1877) has refuted more of the prophetical work of Marx than of George. Capitalism has broken where it was weakest, not where it was strongest, and the proletarian revolt has come in Russia and China, the last places that Marx expected.

As for George, his single tax idea has withered, but it has never been refuted, while his basic principle, that the survival of capitalism depends upon the creation of effective consumer demand, is accepted as axiomatic, not merely in the schools, but also in the executive offices of General Motors and United States Steel. Marx, however, was right in one thing—wittingly or unwittingly, George was promoting the establishment of capitalism on a broader and firmer basis than it had in his time.

Of course, most capitalists didn't believe it and for once they are hardly to be blamed, for the man himself never understood it clearly. George's reach greatly exceeded his grasp. He could adumbrate a highly original idea, but his power of logical analysis was not great enough to enable him to think it through and hammer it to an effective cutting edge. His thinking was always a little fuzzy, which betrayed the hasty and superficial into the delusion that it was essentially mushy.

Marx never made that error. He perceived instantly that the basic Georgian thesis was far deadlier to communism than the preachments of such economists as William Graham Sumner; so he hated George while he regarded Sumner with bland contempt.

Nor was the mistake made by such alert minds as those of Sidney and Beatrice Webb, George Bernard Shaw, J. A. Hobson, Henry M. Hyndman and Herbert Spencer. The last-named, indeed, credited George with having "quietly conquered Parliament" while Hobson's summation was that "Henry George may be considered to have exercised a more directly powerful formative and educative influence over English radicalism of the last fifteen years than any other man." That was written in 1897, so the fifteen years referred to covered the date of publication of the *Fabian Essays,* and therefore Hobson rates George's influence above that of the illustrious society.

Hobson's adjectives, "formative and educative," describing George's influence are worthy of note. He was recognized as a propagandist, not as a philosopher; but no propagandist ever flourished long by preaching a completely empty doctrine. This one's doctrine was far from empty, although its content was never fully exploited by the prophet.

One is tempted to believe that if George might have taken from Marx and applied to himself about half of the harsh intellectual discipline to which the German was subjected, both might have been greater men, perhaps immeasurably greater men. Marx's rigorous intellectuality had ground out of him the capacity to perceive that the structure of the universe is basically illogical. Planck's constant had not yet appeared to set a question mark after all the laws of physics, and Marx was incapable of imagining that moral energy may be as discontinuous as physical.

George, on the other hand, had never been trained as a logician and the scientific process of testing a hypothesis step by carefully controlled step was alien to him. He was an incorrigible jumper at conclusions and sometimes was fantastically wrong; but it is significant that when he was wrong it was by over-shooting or under-shooting his mark, not by jumping in the wrong direction. Marx never jumped; he marched to his conclusion step by severely logical step. Yet by failing to allow for the illogical factor in human nature he marched on Germany but brought up in Russia and China.

Even so, as Barker demonstrates, the American had a much firmer grasp of fundamentals than some of his disciples. Henry George was not a peddler of a panacea, despite Marx's assertion; even in *Progress and Poverty* he did not make the single tax the be-all and end-all of economic theory, and, as his experience widened, its importance in his mind steadily diminished. No doubt to the end he laid too much stress on his theory of rent, but he was acutely aware that the theory was an expedient, not a philosophy. His philosophy rested on the belief that the economic system is a creation of the human mind, not the resultant of universal law. It follows that the system is subject to control by the human mind, and all the inevitabilities of dialectical materialism are as mythical as the amorous adventures of Jupiter and Apollo.

This perhaps is still denied by a small and diminishing Battalion of Death confined almost exclusively to the stuffier rich men's clubs and to the communist splinter party in America; but in general it goes unquestioned, especially since the Hundred Days of Franklin D. Roosevelt, when we actually grasped the economic system and wrenched it around to proceed in a new direction. As Lewis Galantière has somewhat sardonically explained, many of the largest business corporations in America are, in practice though not in theory, more socialistic than half the socialist governments of Europe. It would appal Grover Cleveland if he could know to how large an extent Social Security is now a condition and not a theory, but the average American is not appalled; he takes it as a matter of course because, to quote one who was the antithesis of Cleveland, "we planned it that way."

So when we turn to the record to see what it was that this frantic subversive, this crazy upheaver of civilization actually advocated, the result is rather flattening. The principal items were rent control, public housing (but only where strictly necessary), minimum wages, abolition of child labor, regulation of women's labor, a graduated income tax, regulation of railroad and utility rates, reduction of the 84-hour week then prevalent, old-age and unemployment insurance and, where it seemed necessary, public ownership of public utilities.

All of this has been so far accepted that today not those who advocate but those who oppose it are the oddities, suspected of not being quite right in the head. So it is a temptation to dismiss the whole matter by saying that Henry George was not radical at all and should be listed as a mild progressive, not as one of the Lunatic Fringe.

But it would be a mistake. Henry George was in fact a radical in his own day and the same kind of man is a radical in our day. It is no matter that the specific reforms that George advocated have been justified by the passage of time. Radicalism does not inhere in what a man advocates but in the fact that he advocates it before others have perceived its necessity. Radicalism consists in willingness to take the next step voluntarily, before we are rammed into it.

Check the list of the Georgian proposals and note how many of them gained final acceptance during the Hundred Days. The special session of Congress called by Roosevelt immediately after his first inauguration—it actually sat for ninety-nine days, if you are determined to be exact—enacted a mass of social legislation unprecedented in our political history, not because the politicians making up Congress had reasoned it all out, but because holy hell was breaking loose all over the place and something had to be done. The banks were closed, the national economy was paralyzed, the national guard was fighting milk farmers and mobs were pulling judges from the bench to prevent foreclosures in the Middle West, and eighteen million unemployed faced the alternatives of revolting or starving.

As the event proved, the one program available was workable, so the tottering country righted itself and went on its way rejoicing. Let us not delude ourselves, however, by calling it a triumph of statesmanship. It was not. It was a triumph of one terror over another, the abnormal terror of utter collapse overcoming the normal terror of taking the next step, however obvious it may be.

Salvation of the republic came because at the critical moment Roosevelt had a program; but let no one think that he concocted it in his own head as of the moment. He was undoubtedly a great man, but not that great. He was ready with a program because men like Henry George had evolved it in the previous century, and the whole Lunatic Fringe had been yammering about it for fifty years. The yammering was to no purpose as far as its enactment was concerned, but it was by no means a waste of effort. It exposed the fallacies and weaknesses of the original schemes and afforded opportunity to correct the fallacies and eliminate the weaknesses, not altogether, to be sure, but far enough to make the program viable when the crisis compelled action.

Americans are pragmatists in their estimation of leadership. A man is great if his ideas work; otherwise he has bats in the belfry and none so poor to do him reverence. This is, indeed, an attitude not devoid of reason, but to be wholly reasonable it should be accompanied by a certain temperateness in passing judgment, which it is not; hence the magisterial deliverances of the fathers are comic to the sons, or assuredly to the grandsons, for really original ideas are slow to come to fruition, and a man's true stature is usually revealed, not by his corporeal presence, but by his ghost.

Alexander Hamilton rose from the dead after the Civil War, and was entombed again about the time of the Second World War. Jefferson rose again with Woodrow Wilson, and after a short reinterment during the Harding-Coolidge-Hoover regime, achieved a third advent with Franklin D. Roosevelt. Wilson was obliterated for twenty years but burst his cerements when the guns of the Second World War dreadfully fulfilled his prophecy. The second Roosevelt at the moment seems to be drowsing in Barbarossa's cave, and one shudders to think what agonizing crisis may call him to life again.

Henry George, it is true, is hardly to be listed with any of these, but he, too, walks the battlements of Elsinore because harsh destiny has banged into our heads realization that he was in many respects remarkably right.

Factually and logically, that's that. Yet to say, "so much for Henry George," and drop him there is wretchedly unsatisfactory. It leaves a haunting suspicion that part of the Americanism of the man, and perhaps the most significant part, has been missed. We have heard what his daughter said and we have heard what Dr. Barker said, finding them in substantial agreement, although the daughter is emotional and the doctor is exact. The scientific method in history in such a case counsels us to stress what the exact man says above all else.

Generally speaking, it is sound counsel, but when the effort is to place a man in his historical context rather than to chronicle his doings, a doubt arises. Was Henry George, for instance, more American because he was right, or because he was reasonable?

Some men have been right in their arguments, and yet such unconscionable swine personally that the thought of having to deal with them is repellent to ordinary human beings. The possibility that such men might obtain control of the country is not an idea that will soothe the fears of the faint-hearted because they would infinitely prefer to be ruled by a fallible human being, and pay the penalty for his errors, than live under a Draco who was invariably right, but who was also a monster of ice and steel.

The will of the majority, said Jefferson, "to be rightful must be reasonable," and the words express an attitude—a principle, or perhaps a mere preference, but certainly an attitude—that the American people have held throughout their history as a nation. We are imbued with a profound conviction that the reasonable way of going about changes in our system is the constitutional way, that is, by free choice of the people expressed in balloting uninfluenced by fear or favor, remembering always that "the minority possess their equal rights which . . . to violate would be oppression."

The mildness of spirit that made Henry George adored by his family also made it impossible for him to be a political philosopher of the stripe of Lenin, willing to crush humanity, if necessary, in order to sustain a dialectical point. This mildness may have been sentimentality; the theorists of the Kremlin have no shadow of doubt that it was. But, sentimental or not, it is certainly American. The blood purge is abhorrent to the basic principles of the American system; even the legally defensible hanging of Mrs. Surratt still gives us twinges, and Sacco and Vanzetti are names that we would willingly forget for their memory is scarifying.

So perhaps the thing best worth remembering about Henry George is not that so many of his ideas were right, but that his method was right from the beginning. He did not rely on some supposed inexorable operation of some supposed law of history to bring about the changes that he advocated. He relied entirely on the eventual triumph of the good sense and innate decency of the masses of men.

That is Americanism. The man who advocates reliance on strictly constitutional methods is thoroughly American, no matter what his specific proposals may be; for there is no idea that is un-American *per se* and whether or not translated into action, except the idea that government may derive just power from some other source than the consent of the governed.

So Henry George really supplies to anxious souls a convenient shibboleth by which they may try the quality of members of the Lunatic Fringe today and tomorrow. It is this: do they propose to attain their ends strictly by the means of persuasion and free election, or by some other means? If they propose to abide by constitutional means, they are not un-American. They may be madmen, certainly, but not un-American, no matter how wild their proposals may seem to contemporaries. It is legitimate to defeat them, but dangerous to suppress them; for the event may prove that the apparent madman is really as sane as Henry George.

8

proem

Rulers of powerful and wealthy nations from Marius and Sulla down have found one of their great embarrassments arising from the fact that when the wars are ended the armies come marching home and "the returned soldier element" is difficult to handle. Whether you look at the friends of the Gracchi, at the Grand Army of the Republic, or at the American Legion, the picture is the same—veterans of a victorious army are always disappointed men whose indignation can be whipped up by skillful agitators until it becomes a positive danger to the state.

It is inevitable because during hostilities we always try to stimulate the morale of the fighting men by promising them a great deal more than we are willing to deliver, or can deliver, once the danger is passed. In every army the rank and file are men simple enough to believe the promises, so with the return of peace they become men with a rankling feeling that they have somehow been gypped, and their resentment becomes an uncertain and highly explosive element in the social organization. A typical, although rather mild, manifestation was the proclaimed ambition of the famous Corporal Tanner, of the G.A.R., to drive a four-horse wagon through the United States Treasury, for the benefit of the veterans.

After the Civil War the United States was fortunate in having a safety-valve for the returned soldier element in the empty lands of the West, and in a few years the Middle West, especially, was filled with veterans. But in those early days it was a harsh country and it produced a harsh breed of men. When they found themselves, after battling ferocious climatic extremes, insect pests, and lack of transportation, still subjected to merciless exploiting by Eastern financial interests they refused to submit tamely; as fighting men and the sons of fighters, they reacted violently. Here, in the fourth quarter of the nineteenth century, the great Populist movement took its rise, and in its heyday gave us a Lunatic Fringe that for vigor, color and power far surpassed any other.

The men and women who led this movement were strong but, as a rule, decidedly knobby and gnarly specimens. Their value as intellectual stimulants was enormous, but their esthetic value was denitely low. Only now and then can one find a Populist leader with whom a civilized man would really enjoy spending an evening, but there were some who had more than a blazing dedication to a cause, some who were ingenious, witty, amusing and urbane, that is to say, some with undeniable charm.

In evidence, here follows the tale of:

IGNATIUS DONNELLY

who corroborated Plato and abolished Shakespeare

SCIENCE FICTION WRITERS and people who believe that Bacon wrote Shakespeare's plays are not commonly regarded as threats to the existence of the republic, but today they constitute the last remnants of the mighty army a shock division of which Ignatius Donnelly once led. It was a nondescript army, recruited largely from the dispossessed, and being innocent of discipline or cohesion was therefore doomed to defeat; but it inspired a terror that in retrospect seems fantastic, and its leaders attained in the eyes of the well-heeled and respectable an evil eminence hardly surpassing that later won by Joseph Stalin in minds of the same type.

Donnelly's actual achievements, in the retrospect of fifty years, are so far from lurid that they seem almost pallid. As a young man he read law in his native Philadelphia, abandoned it for land speculation in Minnesota, was flattened by the panic of 1857, joined the newly formed Republican party, went to Congress, served the railroads so faithfully that he was blasted by Elihu B. Washburne and lost his seat after three terms, joined successively the Liberal Republicans, the Greenbackers and the Populists, lost consistently, finally devoted himself to writing, turned out a succession of best-sellers, and died in 1901 aged seventy and like the Thane of Cawdor, "a prosperous gentleman."

In the latter half of the twentieth century it is hard to understand how anyone could hear in this the dreadful grinding of the tumbrils' wheels on their way to the guillotine; but the well-heeled and respectable have an infinite capacity for terror. If no real devil is pursuing them, they can make one out of the most unlikely materials—pasteboard, or cheesecloth, or even Ignatius Donnelly. The well-heeled and respectable are determined to live in a perilous world and if they cannot find it in fact they will create it in imagination.

Not that Donnelly objected—on the contrary, he was happy to go along playing the role of Apollyon and perhaps at times almost believing it. Possibly there were moments when he persuaded himself that the free coinage of silver at the ratio of sixteen to one actually would create a new heaven and a new earth, including such horrors as the destruction of monopoly and the elimination of the leisure class. But he could not have believed it constantly, for three reasons—he was an Irishman, a wit and a poet, and no man who belongs to one

of those classes, not to mention all three, ever believed consistently in a materialistic heaven.

On the other hand, a man gifted with Irish eloquence and
poetic imagination can usually persuade himself to believe
anything, momentarily, including his own possession of in-
fernal powers. So if the opposition insisted upon a devil,
Ignatius was happy to oblige, and did so with a fervor that
was highly convincing.

He was assisted, of course, by the fact that his active life
covered a period that for sordid brutality is not matched in
American history. The national capacity for idealism had
been exhausted in winning the Civil War, and the acquisitive instinct was left without any counterbalance. For a generation after 1865 it ran wild. Its accomplishments in the
material world were prodigious, as the emergence of the vast
industrial nation proves; but they were matched by the enor-
mity of its accomplishments in the realm of the mind and
spirit. Almost every material thing that we are proud of,
and almost every spiritual thing that we are ashamed of,
either originated or was brought to full flower in this period;
it was the moment of triumph of the Hamiltonian philosophy
that "Your people, sir, is a great beast!"

The result was that a man could gain the reputation of a
hideous monster with less trouble at this time than at any
other period in our history. Consider, for example, the platform that Ignatius Donnelly wrote for the Populist party in
1892 and that became the terror of all nervous old women,
male and female, in the country. It included seven planks,
(1) free silver, by which the Populists really meant an elastic
currency, (2) a subtreasury system, (3) a graduated income
tax, (4) government ownership of railways, telephone and
telegraph systems, (5) restriction of "undesirable" immigration, (6) a shorter work week in industry, and (7) direct election of Senators.

With the exception of government ownership every one of those planks is now incorporated in the fundamental doctrine, not only of the third-partyites, and not only of the Democrats, but also of the Republican party under the Eisenhower administration. In fact, the first two, free silver and the subtreasury system, have been left far, far behind. Donnelly never dared advocate anything as extreme as our managed currency and the Federal Reserve System. As for the government ownership of railways, telephones and telegraphs, the effort of both major parties today is not to achieve it, but to avoid having it unloaded upon us. Even the socialists, accepting it in principle, are uneasily aware that it could be done in such a way as to saddle the taxpayers with a mountain of bad debts, and are therefore inclined to proceed with great caution.

Obviously, then, if there was death in the pot it is not attributable to the ideas that Donnelly and his associates promulgated, since all but one have been accepted and have been proved to be not at all lethal. The inescapable inference is that the attendant circumstances somehow invested basically wholesome nutriment with a factor analogous to the toxin that *bacillus botulinus* introduces into otherwise perfectly good canned food.

Among these attendant circumstances were certain social, political and ethical ideas that are no longer accepted universally when they are accepted at all. For instance, from 1865 to 1900 the gravitational theory of prosperity was unquestioned by any reputable business man, and rarely challenged by schoolteachers, college professors or clergymen. That prosperity trickles down from the top was as self-evident to men of that time as the flatness of the earth was to the pre-Columbians. It followed that the acquisitive instinct was listed among the virtues and the possession of money was presumed to be meritorious until proved larcenous; although there was already a growing body of adherents to the opposite faith, that a man's possession of a million dollars was prima-facie evidence that he was a thief.

Above all, there was the faith, little short of sublime, in the *mystique* of the promissory note. Ever since Daniel Webster argued the Dartmouth College case an increasingly emotional value had been accruing to the inviolability of contract. Business on any extensive scale is impossible unless most men can be relied on, or can be compelled to do what they have promised to do. With the coming of the railroad and the telegraph American business was becoming continental in scope, and not merely the exceptional adventurer, but the everyday trader was dealing with people whose faces he would never see and whose honesty he could not judge by his own observation.

So the business world, led by the rising class of powerful industrialists in England, came to regard the sacredness of contract as the Absolute, absorbing all other virtues—naturally enough since their survival as business men depended upon it. It was a short and easy step to extend this sentiment from business to politics and to establish in the minds of business men the conviction that the most damnable of all heresies was advocacy of legislation that would in any way impair the validity of contract.

Within wide limits this was perfectly true. A promissory note had to be good, or business would stall. Legislation that enabled men to escape obligations voluntarily assumed and justly measured was not only bad law, but bad morals as well. But there were limits. Like any other fixed principle, this one could be turned to the uses of pharisaism, that devised ever more numerous and more ingenious ways of respecting it in the letter while violating it in the spirit.

The most effective of these was, is, and doubtless always will be to alter the measure of an obligation without changing its written terms. The standard measure of economic values is money, but it is a shifting standard. The wheat farmers, for example, found often that a dollar was the measure of value of a bushel of wheat when the farmer borrowed a hundred of them, but when he came to pay, it was the measure of value of two bushels. Inevitably the farmer felt that he had been robbed, although he had to admit that the written terms of his contract had not been touched.

Robbery implies a robber and the farmers were not slow to identify the villain as the evil-disposed person who played tricks with the currency. So currency reform of one type or another became the obsession of radicalism for a generation, culminating in the Free Silver movement and Bryan's tremendous campaign of 1896. Conservatives, especially financiers, saw it as an attack on the validity of contract, therefore morally reprehensible; radicals saw it as a defense of the honesty of contract, therefore morally imperative. The conflict was irreconcilable, since both sides battled for righteousness.

Radical opinion was, of course, not altogether wrong. Manipulation of the monetary system did contribute to the ills that beset the country. Jay Gould's corner of the free gold market in 1869, although defeated at the last minute, spread ruin and devastation through Wall Street, and the policies of a good many Eastern financiers undoubtedly drained the productive wealth of the West and South. All this was true, but it was so obviously true that it obscured many other factors that were contributing to the distress of the producers and so it beguiled men like Donnelly into making the tactical error of harping on one string until the public began to regard them as monomaniacs.

It is easy enough today to trace the errors in economics and in logic into which the Greenbackers, the Populists and the Silverites fell; but when the errors have been exposed

there remain two questions which may be more significant
to this generation than is any exploded monetary or political
theory. One of these questions is, why did a program long
since accepted as fundamentally sound generate such genuine
terror in the beginning? The other is, what sort of man was
attracted by a terrifying program?

The answer to the first seems to be that it never was the
specific reforms advocated that appalled the conservatives,
it was the reforming spirit itself. The radicals were subversive characters. They repudiated the theory that acquisition
is praiseworthy in and of itself, and some of them had the
insolence to denounce it as a vice. They were not impressed
by the materialistic triumphs of the years following the Civil
War. In such a development as, for instance, the building
of the transcontinental railroads they were less impressed by
the engineering feat than revolted by the thousands of corpses
of Irish and German and Chinese laborers sacrificed in the
process. They could not deny the marvels wrought by the
titans who industrialized America, but they could and did
assert and frequently prove that the titans had collected from
the public many times what the job was worth. In brief, they
ascribed little or no moral value to success in business.

Unfortunately, nobody else did in his heart of hearts.
Mark Twain's Gilded Age had an uneasy conscience, and it
is precisely the man with an uneasy conscience who is most
infuriated by criticism. The worship of business was a fraudulent cult, and the most devout worshipers had somewhere
at the back of their minds a haunting suspicion that its pretense to embody an ethical and moral system was a hollow
sham.

A great many of them, too, were haunted by another spectre. At heart they had no real confidence in democratic theory, but they lacked the courage to denounce it openly. Thus
they were driven into double hypocrisy—they strove to convince themselves of their own moral superiority all the while

suspecting that they were inferior; and they were forced to pay lip service to democracy although they loathed it. Thus they were exceedingly sensitive to criticism and responded to it with great violence.

There is something very familiar about this. In the second half of the twentieth century frantic denunciation of the direct election of Senators may be archaic, but frantic denunciation of subversives is definitely contemporary; and anyone who thinks that the Hamiltonian theory of the beastliness of the people has no modern acceptance has paid little attention to current events since the days of William McKinley. For this reason Ignatius Donnelly might have stepped out of the Eighty-fourth Congress, instead of the Fortieth, for he fits into the contemporary scene far better than many who were never considered part of the Lunatic Fringe although their ideas now seem more insane than anything proposed by the Populists.

But this character has another touch of modernity. He was a highly successful exponent of Sunday Supplement Science when William Randolph Hearst—frequently described as its originator—was a schoolboy in short trousers. After law, land speculation, politics and farming had all failed to provide him with more than bare subsistence he turned to writing and, like Tom Watson, demonstrated that the pen is mightier than the best sales-talk when the pen is in skillful hands.

Donnelly was a Jules Verne who felt no need to play to the galleries by introducing adventure stories to complicate his fantasies. Fifty years of incandescent political oratory had developed his imagination prodigiously, and five years of hortatory journalism in a weekly, the *Anti-Monopolist*, in which he advocated the Greenbackers' theories, had sharpened his style, so when at the age of fifty-one he turned out his first book he was already an experienced controversialist and a highly competent writer. This was *Atlantis: The Antediluvian World,* an effort to bring Plato's fantasy into the realm at least of probability.

It was astonishingly effective. Donnelly had always been a voracious reader and he had a keen eye for the hidden relations of apparently disparate facts. He had, indeed, more— he had the capacity to create a relation out of his own imagination where none existed in reality and a magnificent ability to ignore facts that told against his theory. Thus he was able to obfuscate any issue he chose to take up so well that the ill-informed were captured, horse, foot and dragoons, while even the fairly well-informed were momentarily staggered and had to think carefully and at length in order to expose his fallacies.

Experts, to be sure, were not taken in by his beguiling account of the continent that had sunk beneath the waves of the Atlantic, but in 1882 experts in a subject so recondite were few. The book sold in such numbers that it rescued the author from his perilous financial situation, and enabled him to devote his time to a new assault on the credulity of the public. This was *Ragnarok: The Age of Fire and Gravel,* a book devoted to the thesis that a comet of immense size and extraordinary density once struck the earth and deposited on half of its surface the stratum of clay and gravel known as hardpan.

It appeared in 1883 and appealed irresistibly to every American who as a schoolboy had devoted part of his time to the unlawful activity of chewing up paper into spitballs which when hurled against a wall produced a satisfying plop and adhered to the surface tenaciously. A sort of cosmic spitball flung against the earth was a concept easily comprehended by the average man, which gave Donnelly a good start.

To this initial advantage he added enough perfectly sound cosmography to impress even the well-educated. He had studied geology and palaentology to such effect that he knew precisely where were the lacunae in the scientists' knowledge and those gaps he proceeded to fill with speculations based on his theory of the comet. It was a baffling method of procedure. A geologist, for example, might be sure that Donnelly's explanation of observed phenomena was all nonsense, but how could he prove it? One must always keep in mind the fact that astronomy has made enormous strides in the past seventy years; when the book appeared in 1883 our knowledge of the structure and behavior of comets, for example, was far less than it is today, and even today it is a reckless astronomer who would flatly deny the possibility of a collision between the earth and a comet of considerable density.

It is the very A,B,C of polemics that it is unwise to try to blast another man for lying when you, yourself, do not know the truth. But to point out that the theory of *Ragnarok* is highly improbable, which is all that a conscientious scientist could say, seemed to the lay public a weak and hesitant form of attack; so the public continued to buy the book in large numbers and to read it avidly, although the scientists fumed, as the political conservatives had fumed when Donnelly was active in their field.

Even in later years when both the man and his books had long been gone as effective forces, critics were inclined to view Donnelly with more irritation than attention. "No one," said John D. Hicks in 1931, almost a generation after Donnelly's death, "could more easily make the worse appear the better reason, and apparently no one delighted more in doing so." * But no one can easily make the worse appear the better reason unless the better reason itself is pretty bad; and in such circumstances there is something to be said for the policy of seeking another, even at risk of stumbling upon a worse.

But in his next endeavor Donnelly moved out of the field

* *The Populist Revolt*, p. 163.

of controversy, for there is no intelligent disputation over a utopia. It was doubtless inevitable that a man of his type should write one but it was not inevitable that it should be good enough to give Edward Bellamy's enormously successful *Looking Backward* a stiff run in the popularity contest; but *Caesar's Column: A Story of the Twentieth Century* did just that. It appeared in 1891, only three years after *Looking Backward,* and it could stand the inevitable comparison.

Three great successes were enough to make Ignatius Donnelly in his later years if not a rich man, at least what they call in Boston "comfortably off." It was a rather odd end for an incorrigible poker into hornets' nests, for poverty and obscurity are the usual fate of such men. But it is by no means certain that Donnelly took much pleasure in his financial success, for his *magnum opus* had flopped most dismally. This was *The Great Cryptogram,* two massive volumes devoted to an effort to prove that Francis Bacon wrote the plays attributed to William Shakespeare.

The reasons for its failure are not immediately apparent. The combination of erudition and ingenuity that went into its fabrication was at least equal to that displayed in *Atlantis* and *Ragnarok,* yet somehow it failed to fascinate the reading public. Donnelly professed to find in the plays an elaborate cipher that Bacon had devised to conceal his authorship from his contemporaries yet making sure that it would be revealed to posterity; the motive suggested was that Bacon thought it undignified for a man occupying his high position to admit the authorship of plays, even the plays of Shakespeare.

Apparently this just didn't go down with the American public. After all, a man capable of writing the plays must have realized their quality; to deny authorship of what one knows are masterpieces is an idiotic act, and Francis Bacon was not an idiot. As for protecting his dignity, half the courtiers surrounding Elizabeth the Great were busily and boastfully turning out lyrics, masques, histories and allegories. The hard-bitten captain of the guard could write of passionate shepherds and scornful shepherdesses without loss of dignity, and if Raleigh could do it with impunity, certainly Bacon, the student rather than the swashbuckler, would have found it easy. So the explanation of Bacon's false modesty was not convincing.

Then if Donnelly's account of how Bacon did write the plays is thin, his argument that Shakespeare did not and could not write them was even thinner, as the average man saw it. This argument, in brief, is that William Shakespeare did not have, and could not possibly have had the learning that is evident in the plays.

This is the argument of a man who acquired learning by slow and painful effort, and who naturally assumes that there is no other way to acquire it. There is no convincing evidence that Shakespeare ever made that slow and painful effort; on the contrary, the sketchy accounts of his life that exist indicate that there simply was not time for him to put in years of study. Hence scholars, especially of the pedantic type, assume that he could not have had the knowledge displayed in the plays.

But the average man assumes nothing of the sort, being estopped in part by what he knows and in part by what he does not know. He knows by the experience of everyday life that there are persons who can pick up accurate information with lightning speed and with no apparent effort, or almost none. We say of a certain boy that he is a born mechanic, and his father, who can hardly drive a nail without smashing his thumb, looks on with bewilderment while the boy sees at a glance the principle of the most complicated structure. How he does it, the father has no idea; but the fact that he does it is undeniable.

So much the average man knows. What he does not know

is the difficulty that most people encounter in mastering any branch of scholarship. Therefore he sees no reason why Shakespeare might not have picked up his enormous store of knowledge here and there much as some boys pick up carpentry with little formal instruction, or none at all. It is idle to tell him that severe intellectual labor is different; having never performed it, he is not convinced.

This is not an effort to prove that Donnelly's argument was unsound, but merely an explanation of why it was not persuasive. It is the rock on which all the Baconian theorists have split. It is certainly true that Shakespeare did not have the kind of learning that Bacon had, but for two hundred years nobody realized that the plays were learned in any way. Milton admitted that Ben Jonson was learned, but Shakespeare, "Fancy's child," could only "warble his native woodnotes wild"; and John Dryden actually tried to inject learning into the plays. Obviously, then, what he had was so far removed from Baconian lore that for generations it was not recognized as knowledge.

So the average man, admitting that what Bacon had may have cost long and assiduous toil in the library, thinks that this does not necessarily apply to what Shakespeare had, which was so different that it took a long time to make men realize that it was learning. Not even Ignatius Donnelly could make any but scholars believe that lack of formal schooling entails blank ignorance.

Nevertheless *The Great Cryptogram* was the culmination of Donnelly's whole career. It is the kind of book that he had to write, the sort of thing to which his type of mind inevitably tends. Unlike the pompous Dryden, Donnelly had a full appreciation of the value of the plays; what he really disliked was the universal acceptance of the idea that Shakespeare wrote them. He disliked universal acceptance of any idea in the intellectual realm. He could not escape the con-

viction that universal acceptance is prima-facie evidence that
an intellectual concept is wrong, and he could not resist the
impulse to try to upset it.

Curiously, this did not extend, in his case, to emotional
concepts. Theodore Roosevelt himself was no stouter defender of "the old moralities" than Ignatius Donnelly. The
witnesses are unanimous in testifying that he was an admirable husband and father, even though as a churchman he
was indifferent, to say the least; born into the Catholic com-
munion, he never accepted any theological system, but
neither did he attack any. Nor did he ever deviate from strict
constitutionalism; he granted the necessity of political authority, and sought to effect his reforms at the ballot box,
never by "direct action," which is to say by anarchy.

The result was that while he acquired the title of "the
prince of cranks," he never outraged the moral sensibilities
of his neighbors, who dubbed him "the Sage of Niniger," the
name of his farm and the site of the ghost town which he had
expected to be a metropolis, but which was killed by the
panic of 1857. In a period when a luxuriant beard was the
accepted insigne of statesmen he went clean-shaven; left a
widower in his sixties he married a girl of twenty-one; and
in his last years he was attracted by spiritualism, but none of
these eccentricities seems to have done him real harm.

Since, then, the issues for which he battled agitate us no
longer, since he apparently did no permanent harm, or accomplished any permanent good, since even his entertainment value evaporated long ago, it is a fair question whether
the evocation of this ancient spectre serves any purpose. As
regards the individual, the answer probably is no. Neither
business men, politicians, editors nor writers of the twentieth century can learn anything about their crafts from Donnelly, although he practiced them all.

But while the individual may have little or no contemporary significance, it does not necessarily follow that the type has disappeared. Indeed, a moment's thought is enough to convince a candid mind that it has not disappeared. We still have what the Russians call "the more demandful," the men who are dissatisfied with all that has so far been accomplished and who look for more and better achievements; and they still irritate the rest of us, especially those who have worked to the point of exhaustion to accomplish as much as has been done. We have more or less discarded Theodore Roosevelt's phrase, and borrowed one from the Muscovites; but by "the Lunatic Fringe" he meant what we mean by the Bolsheviki whom we darkly suspect of being agents of the Communist party. If they are unconscious agents, so much the worse, for then our irritation is mingled with contempt.

Yet the fact remains that the bulk of what Ignatius Donnelly stood for is today accepted as a matter of course by conservatives as well as liberals; so it is evident that the man was one who saw further ahead than most of his generation. More than that, he had the courage to act according to his vision and urged others to action. A man who can see far ahead and who does not hesitate to take the next step is anything but ordinary; he stands out from the crowd like the speckled bird of Scripture, and "the birds round about are against" him. He is a lunatic.

Yet we should be modest in our railing, for again and again posterity has come to account such a fellow the sane man in a lunatic world.

9

proem

When the agrarian revolt really got under way the storm center, in the general opinion of Easterners, was Kansas. To be
sure, winds of gale force struck states as far distant as Iowa and
Georgia, but the outside world clung to the belief that the disturbance was typically Kansan.

One reason, no doubt, was that when the wind began to rise
about 1885 there were still living great numbers of people who
remembered Kansas in 1855 and who therefore tended to associate the name with uproars. But another is the fact that Kansas
did produce not necessarily the greatest, but certainly some of
the gaudiest leaders of Populism. Weaver, the first great hero
of the movement, came from Iowa, and Bryan, its residuary legatee, came from Nebraska, but Kansas supplied a number of figures who played minor roles in politics, but who were terrific
in histrionics.

They are generally remembered as more raucous than persuasive and some were just that, as will appear later. But some who,
when they are remembered at all, are remembered as rowdies,
when they were in fact quite different, being endowed with
clownishness not by their own activities, but by the malicious
humor of their enemies.

This is a point made clear by the tale of:

SOCKLESS JERRY SIMPSON

who showed what's in a name

"HE FACES THE WORLD smilingly," Hamlin Garland
wrote of a congressman whose name, Garland believed in
1892, was Jeremiah Simpson. Later some doubt arose on
that point. Raymond C. Miller, who wrote the Simpson
sketch in the *Dictionary of American Biography*, would not
commit himself. The man was called, and signed his letters,
"Jerry" and for aught Miller knew to the contrary might
have been so christened.

The doubt will never be dispelled. It is supposed that he
was born on Prince Edward Island, Canada, in 1842, and at
that time in that place they treated vital statistics pretty cav-
alierly. No documents have survived to settle the matter
authoritatively, and since Jeremiah, Gerard, Gerald and
Jeroboam are all abbreviated as "Jerry," we are left darkling.
For that matter, his parents may have supposed that Jerry
was an entirely adequate name and have given him that and
that alone.

However, when he said, "he faces the world smilingly,"
Garland knew what he was talking about, for the man was
before him, and the lines about his eyes and mouth when
he was fifty years old were lines of laughter. This is noteworthy, for it is definitely not characteristic of reformers as
a class; as a rule they are solemn fellows and frequently they
are dour; a laughing reformer is something of an anomaly.
Many people, especially among the more important, never
dreamed that Jerry Simpson was one; the mental image of
him accepted throughout the East and in large areas of the

Middle West, including Kansas, was rather like that of Sir
Joseph Porter's British tar:

> His nose should pant and his lip should curl,
> His cheeks should flame and his brow should furl,
> His bosom should heave and his heart should glow,
> And his fist be ever ready for a knock-down blow,

for Simpson was a particularly subversive character in a group
of subversives in the Fifty-Second Congress, the one sitting
in 1892. They were known as the Alliance men, because
they were supported by the agrarian organization known as
the Farmers' Alliance; and it was commonly believed in certain circles that they contemplated bringing about the crash
of matter and the wreck of worlds, for they were definitely
and boisterously opposed to a peasant status for the American farmer. Simpson, in addition to that, was very loudly
opposed to the Santa Fé railroad, a strong and, as he said,
dominant force in Kansas politics.

Most of the Alliance men were, in point of fact, pretty
dismal fellows, honest enough, but utterly absorbed in one
idea, hence dreadful bores except to people absorbed in the
same idea. The effort to portray them as enemies of the human race, or even as enemies of organized society, was nothing more than an example of the high-pressure lying of
extreme partisanship.

Hamlin Garland, writing in the *Arena,* a magazine of considerable influence among the intellectuals in 1892, described
nine men as "The Wedge" of the Alliance in the House of
Representatives. Of these, seven accomplished so little either
for good or for ill that they have been utterly forgotten. An
eighth, Thomas E. Watson, of Georgia, although he seemed
to Garland a rather mild and good-natured reformer in 1892,
in later years did something to justify the reputation of
ferocity attributed to the Alliance men by their enemies.

But even Tom Watson became ferocious many years later, when he abandoned the constructive work of his youth and turned into an anti-Catholic, anti-Semitic, anti-Negro firebrand. Of the whole group Jerry Simpson alone lingers in the memories of men, faintly, indeed, but smilingly, as a really attractive figure in the current Lunatic Fringe.

Even this slight persistence he owes more to the malice of an opponent than to the quality of his statecraft, and to an opponent who, by an odd quirk of fate, was destined to become one of his intellectual heirs. Victor Murdock was the man who gave Jerry Simpson his slight claim to enduring fame. Murdock, then a brash young newspaper reporter, in later years was to go to Congress as one of the wild men from the Middle West, Republican inheritors of the Populist tradition. After a stormy career in the House, he became one of the chief moguls of Theodore Roosevelt's Bull Moose party, the Great Vendetta that assembled among its strangely assorted assets the ideas, and especially the emotions, of the agrarian revolt of the nineties.

In 1888, when that revolt was just beginning, Simpson made an unsuccessful campaign for the state legislature and Murdock was sent to cover the race. Simpson's opponent was a banker much better provided with this world's goods than was Simpson, who naturally endeavored to stand forth as the champion of the poor against the conservative, propertied interests. In one speech he illustrated the point by asseverating that whereas his opponent could easily afford to wear silk socks, he, Jerry Simpson, had great difficulty in buying any. Murdock, reporting the speech, touched it up by making Simpson assert that he wore none; and that gave the candidate an agnomen that has been remembered for three-quarters of a century. Even as Scipio, after the battle of Zama, became forever "Africanus," so, after that speech—or after Murdock's report of it—Simpson became "Sockless."

Not until 1890, however, did Sockless Jerry appear upon the stage of national affairs. In that year the Populists swept Kansas and Simpson, raging against the Santa Fé as the great-granddaddy of all the octopuses in whose tentacles the farmers were writhing, was elected to the House of Representatives from the Seventh District. He was re-elected in 1892, defeated in 1894, and elected again in 1896; but the absorption of the Populists by the Democratic party broke the force of the movement in Kansas. Simpson was defeated in 1898 and spent the remaining seven years of his life in retirement at Wichita.

For a man whose name has lingered so long, and who served three terms in Congress, his legislative record is singularly barren. No important bill was put through by him, no celebrated oration was discharged by him, no successful revolt was led by him. The fact seems to be that he was and is a symbol, rather than a personality. In later years he was seldom referred to as an individual; when his name was mentioned it was almost invariably in some such phrase as "Sockless Jerry Simpson and all that crowd," which is to say he stood as a representative of Populism rather than as a man in his own right.

Yet he was a salty character. Indeed, he was willing to let the world believe that he was an old salt, for in his own autobiography in the official records he mentions that after his parents brought him to this country from Canada in 1848 he "became a sailor at the age of fourteen" and eventually rose to the rank of captain, from the lowly estate of cook. He doesn't mention that he was a fresh-water sailor on the Great Lakes, perhaps because Drummond, the poet, had already taken the romance out of that with his ballad of the wood-scow *Julie Plante* and her unfortunate "Captinne" who came to a lamentable end "wan arpent from de shore." Such associations would have done a man no good in politics, so he never emphasized them; if people chose to assume that he was the kind of sailor who had broiled under a vertical sun on the Line, and had battled the storms that howl around the Horn, that was all right with him.

Nevertheless, Simpson appreciated fully the force of the poet's advice to "all good wood-scow sailor man" to abandon the lakes

> An' go an' marry some nice French girl
> An' leev on wan beeg farm,

except that Simpson made it a nice English girl named Jane Cape, and added a sawmill to the "beeg farm" he purchased at Holton, Kansas somewhere around 1879. Right after the Civil War that state was at once the El Dorado and the purgatory of ambitious young Americans, a rugged land in which fortunes were made with dizzy speed and lost even faster than they were made.

Simpson experienced the full force of Kansas. He went up like the rocket and down like the stick, an experience that jolts a man out of complacency coming and going. No doubt he cultivated his land assiduously, but his great profit came not from his labor, but from the increase in land values with which he had nothing to do. Within five years he was able to sell out for $15,000 cash—the equivalent of perhaps $50,000 today—which he invested in a cattle ranch near Medicine Lodge. No doubt he attended to his cattle business as assiduously as he had the farm, but three years of drought capped by the winter of 1887-8, one of unexampled ferocity even for Kansas, wiped out his herd and left him so loaded with debt that he was glad to get the job of marshal of Medicine Lodge at $40 a month. His ruin, like his prosperity, had no relation to his labor, but was solely attributable to the climate, with which he had nothing to do.

This taught him the extreme vulnerability of the farmer, the primary producer, in a capitalistic economy, and the lesson was driven home by the long series of hard years through which Kansas dragged its way toward the great crash of 1893. Simpson had little formal education, but he was not such a fool that he couldn't see that the cards were stacked against him. When hard and intelligent labor could neither make a man rich nor prevent his ruin, it was idle to tell him that justice prevailed. It didn't and he knew it didn't. He was convinced that the farmer lived under a system deliberately designed to extort from him the fruits of his labor.

Of course he overestimated the element of purpose; the system was accidentally, rather than deliberately, loaded against the farmer, but the effect was the same. The primary producer was, and to some extent is yet, low man on the totem pole of the national economy, and his efforts to better his position were, and are, one of the chief sources of disturbance in national politics.

But Simpson was not wrong in assuming that political action could afford him some relief. Pundits of many varieties have asserted that he was. From William Graham Sumner to Ezra Taft Benson, they have devoted energy and ingenuity to efforts to prove that Populism was fantastically wrong in its basic ideas, therefore doomed to failure from the start. But it is the pundits who talk nonsense, as the history of the past twenty years has demonstrated. It is true enough that political action has not solved the farm problem, but it is idiotic to say that it has not helped greatly. Sixty years after its demise Populism merits the epitaph of Sir Christopher Wren: *Si monumentum requiris circumspice.*

Furthermore at the moment when Sockless Jerry Simpson first appeared in Congress political action was the only means of relief available. Nearly ten years were to pass before Thorstein Veblen set off the first of his dynamite blasts under the philosophical basis of the economics of the schools, and it would take twice ten years for Veblen and his successors to produce enough effect on American ways of thought to make men in large numbers realize that politics was not the only way of approach to the farm problem.

The great trouble with the Populists' program was that no adequate groundwork had been done to open the way for its adoption. It is true that it was not well thought out, including a number of projects that could not possibly have achieved the results desired, and others that, while sound enough in principle, required redesigning in structure. Fiat money, for example, is the only kind of money now current, and it is actually a crime to possess gold coin except under carefully restricted conditions; but to make paper currency practically useful we have had to surround it with a great many safeguards of which the Populists never dreamed. Nevertheless it is fair to say that the Populists' errors were in matters of detail, susceptible of correction, not fatal errors in basic assumptions.

The merit of the movement was the fact that it envisaged the logical next step; and the merit of the men who led it was that they were not afraid to take that step.

This is what gave them their fearful aspect in the eyes of the majority who were afraid. In the perspective of nearly seventy years the striking aspect of the agrarian revolt of the nineties is the mildness of the reforms that it proposed. Populism never questioned the fundamental tenets of democracy, and its socialistic content was very thin. Simpson, for example, is remembered as an advocate of government ownership of railroads; but it is usually forgotten that he proposed government ownership of only enough lines to break the monopoly and establish standards of reasonable freight rates. That is to say, his was the "yardstick" idea applied by Franklin D. Roosevelt to the Tennessee Valley Authority's production of electric power. Jerry Simpson was as definitely a capitalist as his silk-socked opponent; he would have been as appalled by modern communism as any banker, in Medicine Lodge or in Wall Street. He was merely a Kansas farmer crushed in the grip of what was really a vicious perversion of capitalism, and he undertook to do something about it. But in the eyes of the timorous, he who proposes to do something is always a lunatic.

Hamlin Garland touched both the strength and the weakness of the movement in his remark after he had talked to the nine men led by Simpson: "These men corroborated my own impression that great events are moving." Their strength was the fact that great events were moving; their weakness, their inability to estimate and allow for the slow pace of that movement. They pushed ahead faster than public opinion could be moved, and so they failed; but they pushed in the right direction, so their failure no longer seems inevitable, or discreditable.

What made Jerry Simpson the type and symbol of this movement unquestionably was his name. Peffer was his intellectual superior, and Ignatius Donnelly, Tom Watson and Mary Ellen Lease were all far gaudier personalities, but none ever carried a label comparable to "sockless Jerry" as the description of a type. Its spice of humor made it acceptable to his friends, and its touch of contempt made it priceless to his enemies. Above all, it is profoundly American. The barefoot boy is one of the stock figures of the American sentimental, as the barefoot hillbilly is of its comic tradition. A baseball player gained renown exceeding that of equally expert practitioners of his art simply because some sports writer dubbed him "Shoeless Joe" Jackson. In the same way, Sockless Jerry Simpson is a name that sticks to the memory with the powerful adhesion of one of the new plastic glues.

It conveys a false impression, of course. Watching him in the House of Representatives in 1892 Garland noted his "trim, boyish figure and rather scholarly face." At fifty years of age he was still slender, his "hair very black and abundant, but his close-clipped moustache is touched with gray, and he wears old-fashioned glasses through which his eyes gleam with ever-present humor . . . His voice is crisp and deep, and pleasant to the ear."

This is no picture of a crude hobbledehoy, not even when the observer adds, "he is full of odd turns of thought, and quaint expressions that remind me of Whitcomb Riley." Perhaps one of those quaint expressions was his explanation of why he joined the Union army at the outbreak of the Civil War: "Handcuffs and auction blocks for fellows who work don't heave to alongside of justice." Perhaps one of the odd turns of thought was his reminder to the Kansas farmers that while, in the preceding year, they had had to let their corn go for thirteen and fourteen cents a bushel, grain speculators in Chicago got forty-five cents for the same corn. But quaintness and oddity did not prevent him from being entirely presentable to the eye, and an amiable gentleman in his manners. In fact, he was popular in the House, even with some men who violently opposed every idea he expressed. They hated Populism, but nobody could hate Jerry Simpson.

Yet the suggestion of incongruity in the title is not altogether misleading. Sockless Jerry did typify the irruption into the House of a disturbing element, and the fact that he was personally acceptable is irrelevant. After all, Harriet Martineau and Fanny Kemble, both sharp critics of manners, found Andrew Jackson personally charming; but for all that no one in his right mind would claim that Old Hickory was a harmless, neutral element in politics.

As much may be said of Sockless Jerry. He was, in sober

fact, an apparition that struck terror into the very marrow of the bones of conventional politicians, not on his own account but by reason of what he represented. The staid and conservative East really believed that he represented madness. The easily understandable anger of the West was not understood. Instead, it was accounted mass hysteria that was swiftly mounting into mass insanity that must be stopped in the name of reason as well as right.

It was never stopped. It was checked in 1896, largely because the discovery of new gold fields in South Africa and Alaska had suddenly expanded the base of the currency, easing the monetary pressure sufficiently to prevent complete stagnation of the national economy. Nevertheless, the trend of history ever since has been in the direction that the Populists were taking in 1892.

The inescapable inference is that the alarm they aroused was due, not to their insanity, but to the excess of their sanity. They introduced hard realism into political debate, which is always a disruptive and usually a subversive procedure.

"Man shall not live by bread alone, but mostly by catch-phrases," said Robert Louis Stevenson. Certainly it applies to political man in the United States of America. Apparently every great social adjustment is followed by a period in which minor readjustments more or less take care of themselves, or at least are made without any laborious thinking. This period may be prolonged for a good many years and when that happens men, especially those in an advantageous position, quickly fall into the habit of regarding it as normal. But it is not normal, it is morbid. Herbert Spencer, naming a book *Social Statics*, perpetrated a contradiction in terms, for what is static is not social, and what is social is not static. A society may indeed become stagnant, but only when it **is** approaching dissolution. A vigorous, developing society exists in chronic turmoil. Its politics may experience times of relative quiet, but only because attention happens to be diverted to uproars in other fields of activity. If they are really important, such uproars must eventually invade politics, and their appearance terrifies only those who do not, or will not, remember that change is the law of life.

Yet the forgetful are astonishing in number and frequently —one may say habitually—occupy most of the seats of the mighty. Gentlemen whose affairs have proceeded pleasantly and profitably for years tend to become such romantics as might astound Don Quixote. They think that because they are virtuous there shall be no more cakes and ale; and when the inevitable disillusionment comes they are alarmed and aggrieved.

For instance, greenbackism and the free coinage of silver at the ratio of sixteen to one were indeed follies, but only because they could not attain the objective. The objective, the introduction of some elasticity into the currency, was not folly, but stern necessity. Yet even a generation later, when Wilson and Carter Glass introduced elasticity by the instrumentality of the Federal Reserve System, the dreamy mooncalves in the American Bankers' Association fought it to the bitter end.

The still larger objective of Populism, special protection of the farmer against the special hazards of his occupation without the complete abandonment of capitalism, has not yet been attained; but it is no longer seriously denied that he is entitled to special protection, not on account of his superior virtue, but to assure society as a whole safety from the danger of famine. To buttress the farmer's economic security we have adopted many temporary expedients that are admittedly unsound, but preferable to the collapse of agriculture. Any statesman who could come up today with an obviously sound program to save the farmer would be hailed, not as a menace to capitalism, but as its strong defender.

Yet for perceiving this reality and demanding that the country face it Sockless Jerry Simpson and his friends became classical examples of the Lunatic Fringe. It is obvious that their minds ranged ahead of their times, so far ahead that the stark reality they faced was entirely invisible to the majority of their contemporaries; and, of course, any man who sees the invisible is taken to be the victim of hallucinations. But by what process of reasoning can it be demonstrated that it is crazier to be ahead of the times than behind the times? The long and solemn processions of bankers and business men that filed into Washington in 1913 protesting that the adoption of the Federal Reserve System meant embracing socialism look pretty silly now, but only because their protests were overruled and the event proved that the danger had been only in their minds. If they had succeeded, they might be regarded as possessing all the wisdom and virtue of Mark Hanna and his associates who put down Populism.

There is no pleasure in remembering how foolish we were in times past, therefore it is done only under pressure. But the pressures of today are very considerable, enough to cause some minds to wonder where, today, the lunacy lies. It is not beyond human capacity to grasp the truth that in a fluid society such as ours the man who is ready to move, although he may be wrong, has a chance of being right; while the man who stands fast has no chance whatever of being anything but wrong in a mobile society. Sockless Jerry, if he propounded today the ideas that he held in 1892, would be classed as a moss-backed reactionary. But, being the man he was, he would no longer be propounding those ideas; he would be advocating something else too far ahead for most of us to see. So it is probable that in 1957 he would be regarded as just as crazy as ever.

10

proem

It was economic pressure that precipitated the agrarian revolt, so inevitably its leaders devoted their energies largely to arguments regarding the principles and theories of what Carlyle called "the dismal science." Dismal enough most of it is to the modern reader trying to wade through the debates of the time. They are filled with verbose and usually pretty foggy efforts to exploit such things as the theory of rent, the theory of surplus value, the theory of money, the statistical meaning of average, median and optimum, Lasalle's Iron Law of Wages, Malthus on population, Smith on taxation, and all the rest.

Possibly a student of the history of ideas may find a certain fascination in Peffer, droning endless series of figures to a drowsy Senate, for Peffer did have a remarkable facility at drawing the wrong inference from perfectly accurate facts. But for the casual reader, interested only in the human drama, there is nothing but fatigue in following the public utterances of the ablest thinkers among the Populists.

Nevertheless Populism had its moments, the record of which can make even a modern reader sit up with a jerk. Most of them were furnished by relatively minor figures, men and women who thought sporadically if at all, but who felt intensely and continuously. Ideas shift and change incessantly, but emotion is immutable and immortal; indignation, for example, is the same yesterday, today, and forever. Whether it is the wrath of Peleus' son, or the baseball manager shouting, "We wuz robbed!" after yesterday's game, fury is always interesting and diverting. The logic of the Populists may be dreary today, but not their anger.

If you doubt it, lend an ear to the tale of:

MARY ELIZABETH CLYENS LEASE

who was heard—and how!

A HOSTILE PRESS dubbed her "Mary Yellin" under the misapprehension that her name was Mary Ellen. But she was christened Mary Elizabeth. In her palmy days, however, she made little effort to correct the error. She was seeking publicity then, not out of personal vanity, but because her cause needed it, and Mary Yellin is the kind of title people are not likely to forget. Instead of objecting, she made every effort to live up to the misnomer and, as all chroniclers of the time agree, with marked success.

She had a grand time in this world. This assertion is made flatly despite the fact that she was intimately acquainted with poverty, war, contumely and defeat, despite the fact that she never attained wealth, ease and tranquility, and in view of the fact that her eighty years were filled with a succession of uproars. For she was an Irish biddy, dowered with the high emotional potential and the gift of gab characteristic of exceptionally intelligent Hibernians; and to such there is no fate more dreadful than to live through a long succession of days, each a repetition of the preceding one, without incident and devoid of excitement.

No such calamity was visited upon Mary Elizabeth-Ellen, for although she was born in Pennsylvania in 1853 she was only seven years old when her parents moved to Kansas, and in 1860 Kansas was really jumping. Red Legs and Border

Ruffians had been shooting it out all over the place for years and, as the Highland sergeant said of the ill-fated Narvik expedition, "there was never a dull moment." The year after the Clyens family arrived the guerilla fighting swelled into the Civil War, and there was never a dull moment for four years more.

About the girl's childhood next to nothing has come down to us for she was never sufficiently interested in the past to record it, and she never became quite important enough for industrious historians to dig into it while the information was still available. But it wasn't pampered. That is a safe assertion, simply because she grew up in Kansas during and immediately after the war, and anyone who lived a life of luxurious ease in Kansas in those days would have been such an oddity as never to be forgotten. On the other hand, there is no reason to suppose that it was conspicuously unhappy. Hardships there undoubtedly were, but hardships that are common to everyone in the community cause no heartburning in children, and few in adults.

Kansas was still jumping, although in a different direction, eight years after the war, when Mary Elizabeth Clyens married Charles L. Lease, a pharmacist. It was not war this time, it was a financial panic, but it caused devastation in some respects comparable to war. It began in February with "the crime of '73," when the government made gold the sole monetary basis and quit coining the silver dollar, a severe blow to the silver-producing West, and it culminated in September when Jay Cooke, financier of the Civil War, failed and the stock market went to smash. All this was far away from Kansas, but the depression and unemployment that followed hit the state full force. The mystery of the thing was one of its worst features, for nobody understood clearly how it had all come about. Modern economists can explain it as due to bad financing, but it was the best financing known at the time, and people who suddenly found themselves desperately poor for no apparent reason developed a lasting suspicion of banks and bankers.

Perhaps hard times drove the Leases out of Kansas. At any rate, they moved to Texas, where Charles, Evelyn Louise and Lena Grace, three of their four children, were born to them near Denison, the town where, five or six years later, the wife of an employee of the Katy railroad named Eisenhower gave birth to a son named Dwight David.

These years are wrapped in obscurity, for obvious reasons. Any wife of a man who, if not desperately poor certainly is not rolling in wealth, with a house and three small children on her hands has excitement enough without looking outside for it. Mary Lease did nothing to attract attention to herself in Texas, or for a few years after their return to Kansas, some time before 1885. But there is at least one indication that her mind was not so completely absorbed in household routine that she gave no attention to anything else; this is the fact that the fourth and last child, born in Kansas, was named Ben Hur. Since General Lew Wallace's novel was published in 1880, Mary Lease was evidently reading some current fiction, if nothing else.

They settled in Wichita where Charles Lease went into business as a druggist, and Mary began to break away from the normal routine of a housewife. She studied law and in 1885 was admitted to the bar; for Kansas, although it had not yet adopted woman suffrage, was far in advance of most of the states in other rights it granted the feminine half of the population.

Her motives were probably mixed, but one of them was certainly financial, since 1884 marked the beginning of a dozen years of hard times for the farmers. It was a dry year, and crops failed. In 1885 the drought continued, and cattle prices crashed. Both 1886 and 1887 were dry, and the farmers were already in a bad way when the winter of 1887-8 hit Kansas with a ferocity unexampled even in that fierce climate. Most of the herds were wiped out, and cattle-raising never regained a dominant place in the state's economy. In those days if a Kansas married woman could turn her hand to anything that would bring in a little cash she and her family were lucky.

But it is doubtful that the financial motive was the only one in this case. The woman's intellectual vigor demanded an outlet that was not supplied even by the practice of law. No doubt also the emotional pressure of an Irish girl, daughter of a man who had been driven out of Ireland by the political troubles following the Great Famine of 1847, contributed. In any event, presently Mary Lease began to appear on the lecture platform at various places in Kansas with a discourse entitled "Ireland and Irishmen" that was a honey. It dissected the British government without benefit of anesthesia, to the roaring approval of Irishmen and the sons of Irishmen who had fled from political persecution on the Ould Sod. Part of the proceeds of the lectures she turned over to the Anti-Eviction Fund of the Irish National League, then flourishing in America.

The real interest in this episode today is the evidence it affords that if there were no public excitement raging at the moment, Mary Lease was quite capable of creating private excitement of her own. So if her first thirty years were what the modern generation would call a hard life, it does not necessarily follow that it was a miserable existence. The evidence is all the other way. Mary Elizabeth-Ellen grew up in a stressful environment. But she had both the physique and the temperament to take whatever fate might dish out, boredom alone excepted, and that she was not called on to bear. Fragile women might have collapsed under the strain, but there is every reason to believe that she enjoyed it.

However, there was beginning in Kansas a far greater disturbance than she could create by taking Queen Victoria apart on the lecture platform. It was the agrarian revolt that culminated in what was technically called the People's party, but more familiar to us as Populism. Into this movement in 1888 Mary Elizabeth—for some unknown reason then almost always mentioned as Mary Ellen—happily flung all her energies. The Populists were not yet organized nationally, but in Kansas there had grown up what was known as the Union Labor Party, and she addressed its state convention at Wichita to such effect that she was promptly nominated for county office even though, as a woman, she couldn't vote. Kansas did not give the suffrage to women until 1912. She was defeated, of course, but she ran again in 1889, and in 1890 she really took the limelight in a big way.

In that year the redoubtable John J. Ingalls was a candidate for re-election to the United States Senate, and Mary Elizabeth, or Mary Ellen, or in any event Mary, always claimed that she, personally, sunk him. The claim is doubtful, to say the least. William A. Peffer was the real brains of the Populist movement in Kansas and when the Populists won the legislature, which at that time elected Senators, he was the logical choice and was duly elected.

Whoever did it, the feat was a public service, for Ingalls was an empty barrel, capable of giving forth a tremendous booming, but hollow within. First elected in 1873, he devoted his energies for the next seventeen years almost exclusively to the task of keeping Jeff Davis out of the White House. The fact that Davis was in retirement down in Mississippi before Ingalls began, and was dead and buried before he ended, did not bother Ingalls; there was political profit in the issue and the Kansan made the most of it.

The American electorate has always been vulnerable to men of this type. In private life flogging a dead horse is accounted a waste of energy, but in politics it frequently attracts votes in astounding numbers. The dead horse may be any issue once of importance but long since settled—Jeff Davis, the Negro, the Jew, the Pope, the Masonic fraternity and the King of England have all served at one time or another to keep in office some resonant fraud with no claim to public attention save an ability to fan the embers of some ancient hatred long after the dispute has been composed.

The fatality dogging the footsteps of such characters is their tendency to overlook the rise of new interests that are engaging the attention of the people; so the time inevitably comes when the voters, hearing them harping on the same old string, decide—usually quite suddenly—that they are intolerable bores and throw them out in favor of someone who has something new to say. This, and neither Peffer nor Mary Lease, was what actually ruined Ingalls; in 1890 Kansas found itself bored by incessant denunciations of a man already six feet underground, so it threw Ingalls out.

Nevertheless Mary Yellin was very much there when it happened. She is said to have made a hundred and sixty speeches in that campaign and every one of them had something that set the wool-hat boys roaring with delight. One theme, repeated with innumerable variations, was heard not merely in Kansas, but from coast to coast. It was her advice to agriculturists: "What you Kansas farmers ought to do is to raise less corn and raise more hell!" It sounded reasonable to the men in overalls in the prairie fields, and it sounded horribly effective to the men in silk hats in Wall Street.

It sounded dreadfully effective to some Kansans, too, specifically to a young country editor in Emporia. Not in this campaign, but five years later, it was his answer to Mary Ellen Lease that made William Allen White nationally famous. He published an editorial in his Emporia *Gazette* under the headline, "What's the Matter With Kansas?" the tenor of which was that the farmers had accepted her advice all too enthusiastically; they had abandoned corn for hell, and were then suffering from overproduction. Mark Hanna, the Republican boss desperately trying to stop Bryan, saw the article and had millions of reprints distributed over the country. So White, later to become one of the chief ornaments of the progressives, started his career as the foremost bugler of reaction.

But that was to come later. In 1890 the Farmers' Alliance-People's party combination swept the legislature, and Peffer replaced Ingalls in Washington. From the legislative standpoint this was an improvement, for Peffer was intellectually as well as financially honest and a man of real ability; but it is not so certain that it was an advantage politically. Your brilliantly successful politician must be an actor as well as a thinker, for his appearance has much to do with the effect he produces. Peffer was utterly humorless and deadly dull. He was a tremendous worker and he supplied the Senate with masses of accurate information. But the quantities of dry statistics with which he loaded his speeches soon emptied the galleries, including the press gallery, whenever he took the floor.

More than that, his whiskers were as long as his speeches and he had a habit of clawing at them as he droned through endless tables of figures. For all his ability there was a touch of the comic about him that the cartoonists seized with delight. They soon made Peffer in caricature the symbol of the Populist movement, and that symbol undoubtedly handicapped it. It made Populism seem morally earnest, indeed, but dull, dreary and more than a little ridiculous.

Not even the activity of a Mary Yellin Lease could eradicate that impression, for while she was certainly not either dull or dreary, she incurred plenty of ridicule, even when she was technically right. When the Populists captured not only the legislature but the whole state administration in 1893 she was appointed president of the State Board of Charities; but she soon engaged in a deafening row with the Governor, titular leader of her own party, was removed by him, took her case to the courts and licked him. All of which caused the opposition to rejoice exceedingly.

On the platform she was a formidable rather than a winsome figure. "Her chiefest distinguishing gift," wrote an extremely friendly witness, Annie L. Diggs, one of her most loyal followers, "is her powerful voice; deep and resonant, its effect is startling and controlling. . . . She hurls sentences as Jove hurled thunderbolts. . . . She is tall and stately in bearing, well meriting the title bestowed upon her at St. Louis by General [James B.] Weaver when he introduced her to a wildly welcoming audience as 'Our Queen Mary.' "

This is a picture of what at a later date and by less friendly critics would have been called a battlewagon, one that might daunt but would never dazzle the male electorate—and in those days the electorate was exclusively male.

Yet there is merit in it, for the St. Louis incident referred to marked the high tide of the Populist movement, the national convention that nominated James Baird Weaver for President. His military title was no honorary one. It was the reward of distinguished conduct in the field in some of the hardest-fought battles of the Civil War. Weaver had been at Fort Donelson, Shiloh and Corinth, and he first obtained command of a regiment because all his superior officers had been killed. He was no swivel-chair soldier such as were then and are still plentiful in politics. More than that, in 1892 he got twenty-two electoral votes, a record untouched by any other third-party candidate until Theodore Roosevelt won eighty-eight in 1912. So an accolade from General Weaver was no trifling compliment.

At the same time there is reason to believe that even the valiant General experienced some degree of uneasiness in the presence of Queen Mary. Facing the Confederate army he had been a Lion-Heart; facing the great lords of politics, Democratic and Republican, he had never hesitated to speak his mind, indeed he had laid down the law to them. But facing Mary and her like the General seemed to feel that he was outnumbered, and discreetly avoided giving battle. Like every practical politician, he realized that she was a powerful weapon, but he also realized that her recoil was something to be dreaded. In 1896 they parted company on the question of fusion with the Democrats.

Nevertheless, in 1892 she was very useful to the Populists, not in Kansas alone, but in many parts of the country, for wherever she went she made an impression. Her forte was not eloquence; it was her ability to depict the heart of an issue in plain, blunt words. For instance, it was true that some of the Kansas farmers' troubles were attributable to their inability to achieve a compact organization that could speak for them in peremptory tones. It has been the weakness of agrarians everywhere, for were they able to achieve cohesion as a group they could raise a spectacular crop of hell. They could, in fact, take the country by the throat, for they could starve it into submission.

This has always been the secret terror of the financial and industrial powers that for long periods have ruled the United States. Their strength, after all, is derivative while that of the farmers is primary, which, if it could be organized and wielded as a unit, would be invincible. The offsetting factor, of course, has been the sheer impossibility of maintaining cohesion for any length of time in a group deprived of constant, intimate contact among its members. Much of the time the farmer works alone, and until quite recent years he lived alone. Ingrowing suspicion is characteristic of the solitary worker and militates against compact organization. Not until the middle of the twentieth century, when the automobile and the telephone had virtually eliminated the solitude of farm life, did it become possible to hold American farmers together long enough to make effective as simple a thing as an acreage-limitation program.

But agrarian solidarity has always been possible in theory, and even a whispered suggestion, let alone an earsplittingly loud suggestion that it was about to be effected has always struck terror into the bones of people whose living is derived from financial and commercial operations. Even secondary producers, such as industrialists, have always been uneasily conscious of the potential power of the farmer if he ever achieved organization.

Naturally, this has not been shouted from the housetops. The accepted attitude toward the farmer of politicians of all sections and all parties has been one of ostentatious solicitude. But in the eyes of conservatives the deep damnation of the Rooseveltian New Deal was that it carried solicitude into action. Under the circumstances the New Dealers couldn't well do anything else, but they did bring the farming interests together and the farmer obtained a toe hold from which he has not been shaken loose since. All the resentment conservatives feel for the New Deal they felt in the nineties for the Populists; but it was necessary to mask it under a pretense of concern for agriculture.

So when Mary yelled in Virginia that the epitaph of both the old parties would be, "Died of old age, general debility and chronic falsehood," she was striking so close to the truth that politicians shuddered en masse. She was wrong; the old parties did not die. But she was not altogether wrong, for they survived only by getting rid of some of their debility and some of their chronic falsehood.

When she yelled in Georgia, "You may call me an anarchist, a socialist or a communist, I care not, but I hold to the theory that if one man has not enough to eat three times a day and another man has twenty-five million dollars, that last man has something that belongs to the first," she was echoing the profound conviction of millions of Americans, and rich men shuddered en masse. Even those shuddered who were, in the late George Apley's words, merely comfortably off, less than *very* comfortably off. The tremor ran through all who found life easy and proposed to keep it so, and the tremor was productive of unbounded indignation; for nothing makes us more indignant than to have someone agree publicly with our private sense of guilt.

The economic system didn't collapse; but it survived, not because Mary's yelling had no truth in it, but because by 1900 practically everybody was getting enough to eat three times a day, and so not worrying much about the possession of $25,000,000 or more by one man. However, forty years later things once more became as bad as they were in Kansas in 1892. This time the financial system did collapse, and the economic system rapidly followed it to the verge of complete disaster. It was saved only by means of the most tremendous program of redistribution of wealth ever accomplished by a nation not under the scourge of war or in the grip of an iron-handed dictator.

Mary yelling all over the country was striking close to the truth, as when she yelled at the Kansas farmers to start raising hell instead of corn. And all over the country hypocrisy and entrenched injustice shivered.

It wasn't pretty. Indeed, from the esthetic standpoint it was terrible. This grim-faced virago with the foghorn in her throat was a personification of calamity, a flat negation of that sweet reasonableness that, ideally, should characterize government by consent of the governed. No wonder men turned away from the picture, grimacing. And it was not only ugly, but it was also a failure, as far as winning a national election was concerned.

So for a long time it was the fashion among observers of American politics to view Populism as merely a temporary

aberration, getting nowhere and accomplishing nothing under the leadership of people, including the Lease woman,
who were mere futilities, worth hardly even a footnote in
history.

But the passage of fifty years gave us a new perspective
and a more accurate estimate of its importance. The Populist party disappeared after 1896, but it did not die, it was
absorbed by the Democratic party and by a sort of osmosis
penetrated the Republican party. It was a stimulant that
roused both the old parties out of their lethargy. In the
Middle West the Republican party inherited from Populism
a fifth column that transformed the party in its strongest
citadel.

Among Republicans who absorbed the Populist idea were
that William Allen White, mentioned above as denouncing
Lease, and his fellow editor, Arthur Capper, in Kansas. Victor Murdock was another, and others were scattered all over
the great valley—Beveridge, Cummins, Dolliver, Norris,
Borah, La Follette, all the Midwestern group that under the
leadership of Theodore Roosevelt put driving energy into
the Republican party, owed their intellectual emancipation
largely to the shock administered by Populism.

As a political party, though, it was finished when the Democrats nominated William J. Bryan, for he was an orator who
could steal all Mary Yellin's loudest thunder and convert it
into organ music. She knew that fusion meant obliteration,
and she yelled her best against it, to no avail. Weaver and
other influential leaders saw no point in waging a campaign
that could only result in assuring victory to the Republicans.
While they did not regard Bryan as ideal, they thought he
would do, so they closed up shop.

It was not accomplished without turmoil; indeed, it involved some pretty rough stuff. C. Vann Woodward in his
life of Tom Watson has a striking picture of the last moments of the Populist party. At the convention in St. Louis

when a final effort was made to start an anti-fusion demonstration someone put out the lights, and Woodward shows us "the gaunt figure of 'Cyclone' Davis gesticulating under the flickering light of a candle he held aloft; Mrs. Lease yelling from the platform; the mob of delegates in the darkness crying out accusations of 'ugly work' against the fusionists." But it failed, and "twenty-five minutes after the attempt was abandoned the lights were burning brightly in the hall."

It makes a neatly dramatic end to the story of Mary Elizabeth-Ellen Lease, this picture of her yelling from the platform in a futile protest against the darkness inexorably closing in, and it was in fact the end of her career as a national figure. She went out as she came in, still yelling.

But it was by no means her end as an individual. It took more than the collapse of a political party to suppress her. She abandoned Kansas and politics, that is, partisan politics, but she didn't abandon yelling. First she went to New York to write for the *World,* which was campaigning against Bryan, and without doubt she felt that she contributed importantly to his defeat. Perhaps she did, for he was defeated by a very narrow margin.

Her attention, in fact, had turned to wider fields than partisan politics even before the Populist ship went down. As early as 1895 she had published a book with the modest title *The Problem of Civilization Solved.* Its argument was that the stresses and strains of the modern world could be eased "by colonizing the Tropics with Caucasian planters and Negro and Oriental tillers of the soil as proprietors and tenants by occupancy." No nonsense about egalitarianism for Mary!

In New York she found a long succession of uproars to which she could and did lend her voice with considerable effect in decibels, if not in votes. As each came prominently to the fore, she became an enthusiastic and strident advocate of woman suffrage, prohibition, evolution, birth control and Rooseveltian Progressiveism, *i.e.,* the Bull Moose adventure. How she reconciled birth control and Roosevelt's Olympian denunciations of "race suicide," history does not state; but such inconsistencies never bothered Mary.

As for Lease, she had dropped him in 1901. Grounds for divorce, nonsupport, probably solid enough, for one can easily imagine that the mild apothecary had found her insupportable long years earlier.

She died in Callicoon, New York, in 1933, at the age of eighty, subdued somewhat by the weight of the years, but never bored.

She was admittedly little more than a loud noise, but to assume therefore that she counted for nothing is to misjudge the nature of the historical process. As Dunning observed long ago, men are moved to action, not by what happened, but by what they think happened. Whether or not this woman was really dangerous, men thought she was, and her appearance was an apparition that scared half the country into a somewhat more decent consideration of how painfully the other half lives. She added nothing of measurable value either to political thought or political practice; but she did add noise to a genuine and justifiable protest, and as long as the comfortable insist on being at ease in Zion, noise is an indispensable adjunct to the redress of grievances. She had the courage to take the next step before she was propelled into it, which is a great gift. She did not attain either the vision or the courage by any intellectual process known to philosophy, but she had them.

So in retrospect it is pleasant to believe that on the whole she had a good time in this world. She deserved it.

Practically every reform that Mary Lease and the other Populists advocated has been long since adopted. Most of

them have been embodied in the law and the rest are professed ideals of both parties. It is evident that the Populists
had a more accurate idea of the trend of the future than did
the wise and prudent who presided over the nation's wealth
and deplored their lunacy.

The great Populist movement was really great, whether
measured by the numbers involved, the ferocity and dura-
tion of the fighting, or the terror it inspired. Populism, men
say, failed, but the statement, while not altogether untrue,
is inexact. Populism passed. Yet there is ample reason to
believe that its passing was like that of Prince Ferdinand's
father in that it suffered

> a sea-change
> Into something rich and strange,

which our generation identifies as pearl and coral with no
relation to the shipwrecked party that howled through Kansas
in 1896.

Nevertheless, if you strip away the incidentals, the mere
ornament and decoration—or, as some will have it, the blem-
ish and desecration—of the Square Deal, the New Freedom,
the New Deal and the Fair Deal, and get down to the essential thing, the motivation and inspiration of each, you will
find it identical with the motivation and inspiration of Populism.

Indeed, even in matters of detail, a substantial proportion
of Populism has survived. Practically every important item
of the program supported by Ignatius Donnelly and Sockless
Jerry Simpson is now either the law of the land or embodied
in the most recent platform of both major parties. For fourteen miserable years we adopted even Carry Nation's program, to our great discomfort.

It can be argued and it is being argued that Populism, far
from having failed, has succeeded all too well. Nomination
by primary, for instance, has had in some instances an effect

opposite from the one expected. While it has justified itself on the lower levels of politics, it has made campaigning for high office so burdensome and expensive that no man need enter such a race unless he is rich, or has friends who will supply him with a huge campaign fund. Yet the belief of the Populists was that the primary would throw open a political career to anyone, not merely to friends of the political bosses. It is true that a modern candidate cannot rely implicitly on the bosses; but in lieu thereof he must follow the Scriptural injunction, "Make to yourselves friends of the mammon of unrighteousness," which is no great improvement. Yet for all that, the primary is firmly embodied in our political system.

So is the direct election of Senators, so is the graduated income tax, so is the principle of regulation, not merely of public utilities, but of all "natural" monopolies. Complete governmental control of the currency is no longer questioned, even in Wall Street; and the Stock Exchange itself has come around to the view that anyone who issues securities for sale to the public should be held to a strict accountability if he misrepresents them in any important particular.

All these things were derided when they were urged by the Populists, and by the Populists' residuary legatee, Bryan, sixty years ago. Yet one by one they have been adopted because, one by one, they came to seem inevitable.

Most spectacular of all the changes that Populism urged in vain, but that have since been effected, is that in the status of the farmer. Populists as a rule loathed and denounced employing the power of the state to protect certain favored industries; yet they made every effort, and strove in vain, to establish agriculture as a protected industry. It is the second generation after them that has made long strides in that direction, and again it was a question of bowing to the inevitable. The collapse of the whole economy following the panic of 1929 brought us face to face with the grim fact that if we allowed the farmers to starve first, the rest of us would starve thereafter, and speedily.

Unfortunately, as regards this problem, the passage of time has brought small increase in wisdom. Our efforts to protect the source of our food supply against the boom-and-bust gyrations of the price system have been anything but brilliantly successful, perhaps because of our reluctance to try to make a distinction between true primary producers and speculators in agricultural commodities. It is difficult to state in terms of statute law the exact difference between a farmer and a land operator who does no farming himself, but hires farmers by the dozen or by the hundred to work his land.

Nevertheless, the Populists have made their point. It is now admitted that the nation, for its own protection, must take measures to protect its supply of agricultural commodities. The policy may be socialistic; but any other policy is suicidal, and even the most reactionary Wall Street banker would rather be a socialist than a suicide.

The question then arises, Why did it happen that so much of the Populist program has been forced upon us, not by logical argument, but by the grim, relentless pressure of events? Did they, in fact, excel all others in wisdom and virtue, or at least in perspicacity? The assumption would be hard to maintain. It is clear, now, that they were often wrong, especially in the methods they advocated—as, for instance, greenbackism—and occasionally in their objectives. Sometimes when they became, to adapt Disraeli's phrase, inebriated with the exuberance of their own verbosity, they were worse than fantastic, they were downright idiotic. No, their individual superiority is not the answer to the survival of their ideas.

It goes back, rather, to their correct alignment upon the fundamental base of the American republic. That base is the assumption that men are endowed by their Creator with certain inalienable rights, among which is the pursuit of happiness; and that to secure these rights governments are instituted among men, deriving their just powers from the consent of the governed. It follows that governments are not masters, but merely instruments in the hands of men, instruments designed to secure, among others, their right to the pursuit of happiness. This function supersedes all others and whatever policy, or philosophy impedes the discharge of this policy is a false policy or philosophy, from the American standpoint.

As a matter of abstract theory it is perfectly conceivable that this is not the best base on which to found a government. In the course of generations to come the American people may discover some nobler and firmer principle on which to rest their political structure. But it has not happened as yet, and in the meantime this is the base of our republic and only those political concepts that rest squarely upon that base may be expected to stand up indefinitely. The merit of the Populists was that for all its nonsensical excrescences, the center of gravity of their program was as directly aligned with this base as an architect's strong tower is aligned with bedrock.

That, and not their superior wisdom and virtue, is the secret of the final triumph of their cause.

11

proem

Like chaff before the wind Populism, as a political party, was whirled away by the blast of emotion created by a popular hero idolized as no American politician had been since Andrew Jackson and as none was to be again until the second Roosevelt and Eisenhower. The surprising title of one of Vachel Lindsay's poems was also the dirge of the Populist party; that title is, "Bryan, Bryan, Bryan, Bryan," and it was the Chant of the Millions in 1896.

But while everybody has heard of the Great Commoner few remember the man who was Bryan's intellectual armorer in the campaign of 1896—few indeed know that he ever existed, although he outlived Bryan by eleven years, and was far more fantastic than the orator of the Cross of Gold.

Yet he was of such quality that to call him a man of vision is faint praise. He was always rather uncertain of what lay under his nose, but when he was approaching the age of eighty his imagination developed a sweep so prodigious as to deserve being called apocalyptic, for he looked into the future as far as archaeology looks into the past.

It is true, sadly true, that the history of American politics is concerned with a tremendous proportion of dull fellows; but not always. For an exception turn your attention to the tale of:

COIN HARVEY

who understudied Cheops

HOPE WAS HIS middle name and he lived up to it, which was enough in a cynical world to enroll him in the Lunatic Fringe even had there been nothing else to set him apart from the grave and prudent. But in addition to that, he laughed at successful business men, ran for President on a third-party ticket and, like Cheops of Egypt, hoped to achieve immortality by building a pyramid. He was distinctly un-American and to a public committed to the theory that all who are not American are lunatic there was no shadow of doubt about his case.

Nevertheless William Hope Harvey had a tremendous influence upon the course of American political history. It can be argued with some plausibility that he influenced it more profoundly than any other individual between Abraham Lincoln and Woodrow Wilson, because it was Harvey who gave a cutting edge to William Jennings Bryan's philosophy, and Bryan's first great campaign prepared the way for the monetary reforms embodied in Wilson's Federal Reserve System.

Yet Harvey's own story is a monotonous chronicle of misdirected effort leading to spectacular failure. He made at least two fortunes, but lost one and gave away the other. As a candidate for President of the United States he got eight hundred votes. As a pyramid builder he left nothing but a group of curious ruins in a forlorn recess of the Ozark moun-

tains in Arkansas. His chief reward for his public services
was abuse and ridicule. But he could not only take it, he
could dish it out too. His own abuse and ridicule of the high
priests of the great god Mammon were so deadly that they
dispelled forever the odor of sanctity with which Mammon's
idolaters had thurified themselves for a generation and threw
into them if not the fear of God at least a healthy respect for
the wrath of the people.

Born in 1851 near Charleston in what was then Virginia,
but is now West Virginia, he started life as a schoolmaster in
his native state, later went to Ohio and studied law, then
drifted west and practiced in Denver, Colorado. By degrees
his law practice concentrated on land law and eventually
developed into dealing in real estate at which he prospered
famously; but the panic of 1893 caught him overextended
and he was wiped out. He went to Chicago and got a newspaper job, but his chief interest never was in the day's news;
it was in trying to understand what had happened to his
fortune.

It was obvious that what had sunk him was lack of ready
money. If he had been able to hang on he would have been
a rich man; for in later years the property he had owned increased enormously in value. The puzzle was, why had
money suddenly become fatally scarce in 1893? As Harvey's
ideas on this subject clarified he presented them in a series
of newspaper articles which he signed with the nom de
plume "Coin" and in 1894 he elaborated these ideas into a
book with the title *Coin's Financial School*. It sold two million copies in the first year and in the long run its total sales
are estimated at between five and ten million.

Even sixty years later these are figures to make a publisher
gasp. It is true that the book was cheap; it was printed on
poor stock and bound in yellow paper covers; it sold for a

quarter, but it must be remembered that a quarter in 1894 was easily the equivalent of a half-dollar today, while the population of the country then was less than half what it was in 1950. To gain an adequate idea of the magnitude of Harvey's publishing achievement the figures must certainly be doubled. A contemporary author who could issue a paperback nonfiction title at fifty cents that would sell four million copies the first year and between ten and twenty million all told would be regarded as a miracle worker of the first rank.

Add to this the fact that the subject was not only economics, but what is perhaps the driest branch of the "dismal science," the theory of money, and the feat becomes all the more remarkable. It is without parallel in the history of American book publishing.

The explanation is that *Coin's Financial School* was not the sober dissertation that its author thought it, but a terrific satire. Coin was well aware that his method was satirical, but he seems to have had no suspicion that so was his matter. Neither did his readers. Even the more intelligent who recognized that his "school" was entirely fictitious assumed that his doctrine was sober fact, and to this day there are many who cannot see what is wrong with it. And they enjoyed reading it.

The prodigious effect of the book was due to its timing. In 1894 the country was in such distress as it did not experience again until 1934. People were starving in the midst of plenty. In the presence of enormous demand, indeed desperate demand, production had fallen to a catastrophic level and there were no jobs for able-bodied men in acute distress. In the circumstances, anyone who offered a credible explanation of this mystery was bound to command attention and Coin's explanation was simple, lucid, persuasive and highly entertaining. Naturally, a suffering people snatched at it, and the fact that it was inadequate did not appear for a long time.

The method of presentation was admirably adapted both to the subject and the time. Coin imagined a school in Chicago in which he explained the principles of finance to financiers, economists, merchants and journalists, calling them by name. The book was crudely, but effectively illustrated; Coin was portrayed as a young man, or, rather, a schoolboy dressed in an evening coat and knee-breeches, like an ambassador at the Court of St. James's, who stood before a blackboard expounding monetary theory to such dignitaries as Joseph Medill, editor of the Chicago *Tribune*, Lyman Gage, president of the city's biggest bank, Marshall Field, Franklin Mac-Veagh, Phil D. Armour, Potter Palmer, H. H. Kohlsaat, Levi Leiter and Leander McCormick, all of whom were not merely big business men, or revered authorities on economics, but in the very top flight of such tycoons.

All these men had been giving out ponderous and impressive statements on the depression, very much as Herbert Hoover, Andrew Mellon and John D. Rockefeller did between 1930 and 1932; and their statements were basically as idiotic. Harvey had studied them carefully, and incorporated them in his book. He quoted his victims' own words, except that he put them in the form of questions addressed to the young schoolmaster, which gave him the opportunity to make devastating replies.

The fury of the men so impaled, and especially that of their worshipful admirers, "the little brothers of the rich," was superheated by the fact that they could not deny the statements attributed to them, for they were on record in the newspapers, magazines and other public prints. They could only denounce the insolence of anyone who presumed to make them look ridiculous.

An example of the sort of retort to Harvey that was thought adequate at the time is the comment of the usually dignified *Nation* in its issue of June 6, 1895. It discovered that certain statistics quoted by Coin Harvey in one of his arguments were taken from Sir Archibald Alison's *History of Europe,* widely accepted as a standard authority. The *Nation* devoted more than a column to an argument that Alison, although a reputable historian, was not a reliable statistician, and ended with the comment, "The true answer to the entire operation is the same that has been applied to so many of 'Coin's' other statements: 'The boy lied.'"

Yet it is obvious that if anybody lied it was Alison, not Harvey. When a man in good faith quotes an authority generally accepted for years the man is not a liar even if the statement is false. In this case it is by no means proved, in spite of the *Nation,* that the original figures were false, and the interpretation that Harvey gave them has since been amply justified.

The point is that in 1894 the monetary system of the United States was rigidly bound to gold, and an inelastic currency does facilitate crooked manipulation. That had been abundantly proved in 1869, when Gould and Fiske actually cornered the supply of gold in the free market. At the last minute the corner had been smashed by action of the government in releasing gold not in the free market, but held in the Treasury; but although the attempt failed, it demonstrated the feasibility of robbery on a colossal scale by manipulation of the currency supply.

It was still feasible in 1894, and everybody knew it. True, no such spectacular villains as Gould and Fiske were apparent in the picture, but the suffering millions suspected that the reason was that the money lords in Wall Street had learned discretion, rather than morality. Certainly something had happened to render the money supply inadequate to the needs of commerce and industry. Crops were abundant, but people were starving while factories stood idle. Those grim facts stared everyone in the face, and they could not be explained by any act of God or of the common enemy, for God had sent the rain and the sunshine and there was no overt common enemy.

So if Coin Harvey oversimplified the situation, as he certainly did, there was nothing implausible in his argument. In fact, it was sound, as far as it went; its fallacy lay in its omission of certain factors of profound importance that were influencing the course of events quite as strongly as the things he did mention. His assertion was that the trouble was attributable to the rapacity of high finance assisted by an archaic monetary system. As a matter of fact, high finance had been rapacious and the monetary system was archaic. That was not all that was wrong, but that was part of it.

The gentry who delighted in calling themselves Captains of Industry had not created the conditions that enabled them to drain the products of productive labor away from the Middle West, but they took full and effective advantage of those conditions. For a time the system was vigorous enough to stand the drain and the Captains of Industry were quick to award to themselves credit for the prevailing prosperity; but when the drain became intolerable and the system broke down, they thought it an outrage that they should be blamed for the ensuing hard times. They denounced Harvey and people like him as ignorant demagogues deliberately misleading the people.

That they were ignorant is not to be denied, but that they were a whit more ignorant than the tycoons who denounced them is doubtful. It is true that *Coin's Financial School* exhibited no adequate comprehension of the profound changes that were affecting the national economy, but it showed up with startling effectiveness the equal ignorance of those who had been posing as the omniscient overlords of business and finance. When pomposity steps on a banana peel and takes a spill, it is only human to laugh; and the country laughed loud and long when this book appeared.

The reception given the book consisted almost exclusively of delighted laughter on one side and wrathful sputtering on the other. Only here and there did an exceptionally astute critic observe that the fundamental weakness of the work was its failure to offer any effective remedy for the ills it diagnosed; but even such unusual minds were not prepared to do what they criticized Harvey for failing to do.

A generation was to pass before a school of economists led by the Englishman, Keynes, was to begin trumpeting the theory that the great industrial nations have passed from an economy of scarcity to an economy of abundance, and therefore the problem of distribution takes priority over the problem of production. In 1894 the most learned savants in America had not conceived that idea and certainly the relatively ignorant Harvey had not. If he had, it would have wrecked his whole system of thought.

For like most of his generation, he was committed to two fallacies. The first, and greater, was that the ills that beset the country after 1893 were all, or almost all, attributable to defects in the monetary system; the second was that the chief defect of the monetary system was the narrowness of its metallic base. Hence his remedy was to broaden the base from gold alone to gold and silver at the arbitrary ratio of sixteen to one—that is to say, that it should be the law in this country that one ounce of gold is worth sixteen ounces of silver, regardless of what the world market did.

The fact was, of course, that the defect of the monetary system in 1894 was its lack of the power to expand and contract in response to the needs of business; and rigid adherence to any metallic base would destroy that elasticity. In 1913 we corrected that defect. But then came 1929 with its shocking revelation that a defective monetary system had been only one, and a relatively minor, weakness of our economic system. Distribution was a still unsolved problem, and an admirably elastic currency did not prevent a crash worse than that of 1893.

So the theoretical side of *Coin's Financial School* holds little interest for the twentieth-century reader except one with a special devotion to popular mythology. Even at the time, this was clear to the keener American minds. Joseph French Johnson, for example, the father of the modern business school, reviewed the book for the *Annals* of the American Academy of Political and Social Science in 1895. Unlike the *Nation*, he did not waste time calling the author a liar; on the contrary, he admitted the substantial accuracy of his facts, but pointed out the glaring defect in his theory: "Having proved to his satisfaction that evil results from the scarcity of money, he assumes that the merits of a policy which increases the money supply need no demonstration. He begs, therefore, the real question at issue. . . . He does not prove and really does not try to prove that the free coinage of silver will help matters."

In short Harvey, damned for being riotously imaginative, was not imaginative enough. Assuming that silver is approximately sixteen times as abundant as gold, he took it for granted that its monetization would furnish a specie circulation adequate for all possible legitimate needs of the country. He could not envisage a time when we would be spending every year on one item of the cost of government, armament, almost 150 per cent of the total supply of gold coin and bullion in the country. But in 1955, with twenty-two billions of gold in our possession Congress appropriated thirty-two billions for armament alone, to say nothing of the other expenses of government.

We have partially overcome the difficulty by a series of expedients going far beyond the monetary system. We have attacked the whole problem of distribution, on the theory that it becomes dominant in an economy of abundance, as the problem of production was dominant in an economy of scarcity; and although we have not yet solved it, we have made progress in a dozen ways never dreamed of by Coin Harvey.

It is interesting to note, however, that in dealing with the monetary system we have adopted successfully one expedient well known to Harvey, but which he rejected as part of the discredited Greenback movement. The Greenbackers were proponents of fiat money, that is to say, government promises to pay but bearing no interest and backed by no security other than the government's promise. Such notes—they got their name from the fact that the face of the note was printed in black, the back in green ink—had been issued during the Civil War and, because the quantity was limited, with fair success.

The Greenback party, led in 1880 by the same General Weaver who later headed the Populists, proposed to expand the currency by issuing such notes at harvest time on the security of agricultural products. Their opponents charged that this was the most completely lunatic of all monetary theories; it meant, they said, that "Farmer Corntossel wants to use pumpkin leaves for money."

Today the staid, conservative, intensely sane Federal Reserve System does exactly that. At peaks of commercial activity, as when the crops are being moved to market in the fall, credits based on farm products in storage or in transit provide an expansion of the money supply to meet normal needs, and repayment of the loans provides for its automatic contraction when the emergency is over. In short, pumpkin leaves—oh, well, then say carloads of wheat and bales of cotton—make very satisfactory money at harvest time. The wildest insanity of the Greenbackers was sound in principle, and seemed lunatic only for lack of means to apply it.

Harvey, of course, was not a Greenbacker. He was a silver man who scorned the theories of the Greenbackers as bitterly as any Gold Bug did. He agreed with Old Bullion Benton that only hard money could be good money; he simply contended that silver is as hard as gold. It was his singular destiny to be lunatic enough to be wrong in the eyes of his contemporaries, but not crazy enough to be right in the eyes of posterity.

Coin Harvey would have been a powerful influence on the thinking of the country in any event, but he might never have been regarded as a towering menace, except for one convert, to wit, William Jennings Bryan. After his nomination on the Democratic ticket in 1896 the candidate for President confessed to a friend that his knowledge of the money question was inadequate, and the friend in all seriousness recommended books by half a dozen learned and revered economists and then, rather as a joke, added to the list *Coin's Financial School.* As the campaign developed he was perturbed, indeed scandalized, to find that Bryan in his speeches discarded the heavy tomes of the savants and went right down the line with Harvey. He never admitted his debt to the man, but his argument on any phase of the money question was almost always identical with Harvey's.

This has frequently been cited as proof of the shallowness of Bryan's thinking but it may just as logically be held up as proof of his superb quality as a campaigner. Few American politicians, perhaps none since Lincoln, understood the mind of the average man as completely as Bryan did. Since it was the average man to whom he was appealing, he sought arguments that would appeal to that mind and Coin Harvey supplied them in an abundance and with a clarity not approached by the learned doctors who, like the traditional sermonizer, dived more deeply into the subject, but also stayed under longer and came up drier than the chatterbox Harvey did.

Bryan was trying to win an election, and for that purpose convincing the university faculties was far less important than convincing the groups around the cracker barrel in country stores. He came so close to doing it that only desperate work and floods of money in the closing days beat him by a popular majority of 600,000 in a vote of 13,500,000. The narrowness of the margin ended forever the smug complacency of the Gilded Age and marked the beginning of the somber transition of the business tycoon in ten years from a Captain of Industry to a Malefactor of Great Wealth in the eyes of his impecunious neighbors.

The shallowness of Bryan's thinking is proved, not by the fact that he used the weapon that Coin Harvey put into his hands in 1896, but by the fact that he abandoned it thereafter. Twice afterward he tried, but never again did he come as near to success; nor did his party come to power until it found in Woodrow Wilson a leader whose thinking went in the same direction as but far beyond Harvey's.

Most of the profits of the Financial School were dumped into Bryan's campaign chest, although Harvey was doubtful of the policy of fusing the Populist and Democratic parties. He was not a partisan. He was a man of one idea, and it mattered little to him which party won, provided it would advance the idea. Eventually he became convinced that neither of the major parties would ever revive bi-metallism, which explains the absurd adventure of the Liberal party in 1932, with its 800 votes out of a total of 38,000,000. (Women by that time were doubling the number of voters.)

The writing of *Coin's Financial School* was the one great peak in William Hope Harvey's career. He continued to write, but he had no more to say. He was an excellent diagnostician, but he had no skill at treatment. Nevertheless, through sheer force of personality he retained something of a following to the end of his life and as a magazine writer and lecturer was occasionally heard of for many years.

This is interesting, since he was not endowed by nature with any of the physical attributes commonly associated with power. Bryan, for instance, looked more like a statesman than all of the abler statesmen of the time put together—a big man, physically, with the head of a Roman emperor and a voice whose organ tones were the wonder of the world. Harvey was of medium height, slender and in youth rather good-looking, but in an insignificant way; as he aged he became scrawny and his last photograph resembles the man with the pitchfork in Grant Wood's famous painting, "American Gothic." His speaking voice was not memorable, nor his stage presence arresting, and he has left no record of golden eloquence.

But he was ever a dreamer of golden dreams, which he could put into words so clear and plain that the dullest could understand. To the weary, the dispossessed, the frustrated, he was the man with an explanation and so the embodiment of hope. Living up to his middle name he never failed of some following, however slender, however frail.

Above all, throughout his eighty-five years he retained the dignity that attaches to the Disciple Nathanael, "an Israelite in whom is no guile." Avarice or even mild self-interest had no place in the character of William Hope Harvey. Even his last astounding project promised nothing whatever for Coin Harvey but was designed for the benefit of a generation so far removed in the future that the date of its advent must be computed in geological time. If there was a trace of self-interest in this scheme, it was no more than a wistful hope that in the dim, distant future archaeologists might know that a man named Harvey once lived, as we know that a man named Tut-Ankh-Amen once lived in Egypt.

This project was the erection of a structure in the most durable form known to architecture in which should be deposited records of contemporary civilization. The site chosen was at Monte Ne, Arkansas, in the Ozark mountains in a valley that Harvey believed was destined to be gradually filled by erosion. There he would build a pyramid sixty feet square and a hundred and thirty feet high in which the records would be sealed. Then when earth brought down by erosion from the surrounding hills had filled the valley until only the steel tip of the concrete pyramid appeared above the surface, men of that day might excavate it and learn from its contents what life had been like in that valley thousands of years before.

Lunatic? Doubtless, but not sordid, not small—like that of old Cheops, it was an imperial lunacy. It fired the imaginations of an astonishing number of people who contributed money to this dream. They actually sank a shaft to bedrock, and they constructed an amphitheater with seats of stone; it was in that amphitheater that the remnant of Harvey's following gathered to nominate the octogenarian for President in 1931. But already the woes of 1893 had swept upon the country again. It was no question of an inelastic currency this time, for the currency had been made elastic beyond anything dreamed of in *Coin's Financial School.* Errors and follies of which his thinking had taken no account were responsible this time and far more and greater work than he envisaged had to be done.

But hard times cut off contributions and the work was abandoned. Depression still lay heavily upon the land in 1936 when Harvey died, and the fragmentary structure stands there today, an astonishing ruin as out of place in the Ozarks as anything could be. It is without doubt an absurdity, but there is none the less a touch of grandeur upon it, a hint of thought ranging beyond time and space, scornful of the petty hopes and petty fears that fever us, defiant of the abyss of oblivion.

In that it symbolizes its creator. Nobody would list Coin Harvey among the great Americans, but there were elements of greatness in him, and it was to these elements that the people responded. He had the courage to revolt against the hero worship that raised the titans of the business world above criticism; he examined the facts as they were known to him and from them drew logical conclusions; he had the courage to take the obvious next step and to urge it upon his contemporaries; and he had the character to subordinate his own material interest to the general welfare.

Grant that he was handicapped by his ignorance of the history and theory of economics. Grant that his imagination was not sufficiently powerful to devise adequate remedies for the ills that he identified correctly. Grant that he was a child, and not even a very bright child, in the realm of practical politics. Nevertheless, with all these flaws, he stands out as a superior man, and it was not the flaws, it was the superiority that the people instinctively recognized.

Perhaps the ruins in the Ozarks are not more absurdly misplaced than was William Hope Harvey in the environment into which he was born. Yet about him as about them, there is a touch of grandeur, a reminder that if our thoughts creep, earth-bound and slow, it is because we will have it so, not because we are bound by any iron law of nature; for the mind with the courage and energy to try it can always soar.

12

proem

It is not among members of the Lunatic Fringe that a judicious inquirer spends much time seeking for great men. It is characteristic of them that they possess some element of greatness, but it is also characteristic that they lack the poise, the balance of qualities that lifts a man to the highest eminence and that in American history is uniquely exemplified in George Washington.

But occasionally it happens that not the men, but the times are out of joint, in which case it is sanity that becomes abnormal. In Bedlam the man possessed of all his faculties is the oddity.

Some man with a sense of humor who aspires to the Ph.D.—assuming that there is no contradiction in terms here—might do a brilliant and hilarious dissertation on the times and places in this republic when and where mass hysteria has proceeded to such lengths that sanity became reason enough for committing its possessor to an institution. He would start, of course, at Salem with the witchcraft trials in 1692, and after making pretty much the round of the country—Washington, D.C., being excluded as ineffable—might reasonably wind up in Massachusetts again on the day that Boston elected a convict then behind the bars as her mayor.

The course of this peregrination might take him to Chicago more than once, but it would certainly take him there in the year 1892. Then he would discover one conspicuous member of the Lunatic Fringe who, in defiance of all rules, was a genuinely great man.

Which is abundantly proved by the tale of:

JOHN PETER ALTGELD

who is dead, but will not lie down

ONE WHO denounces the hog-trough without having been able to plant a single hoof therein arouses little real resentment among the swine. They can attribute his ill-humor to envy, and dismiss him with fairly good-humored contempt. But one who has demonstrated an undeniable capacity to obtain his full share of the slop despite the jostling of the herd, and then denounces the trough is regarded as a traitor to his class and is the target of unbounded indignation.

The reason is plain. The convenient explanation of envy will not serve in such a case. Denunciation coming from one who has proved his ability to survive the trampling destroys the illusion that moral superiority attaches to mere survival; which is naturally resented by those who have no other claim to moral superiority.

The intensity of the hatred aroused by John Peter Altgeld in the last quarter of the nineteenth century is explicable only on the ground that he had been a successful business man before he became a political and social reformer. His was a typical American success story spoiled in the end by intrusion of a realism that in the Chicago of those days was far more un-American than the Communist Manifesto; and it aroused a horror that was perfectly genuine.

Altgeld's admirers, of course, are not content to call the quality that distinguished him by as prosaic a name as realism. They prefer Vachel Lindsay's words: "The valor that wore out your soul in the service of man." Valor it certainly was, and that it served mankind is hardly open to doubt;

but that it was intended primarily to serve man is questionable. It may be argued with great plausibility that what Altgeld really tried to serve was common sense, and that his service to humanity was incidental to that. Looking with a clear and steady eye on conditions existing at the time he saw that many of them were harmful not only to

> The widow bereft of her crust, and the boy without youth,
> The mocked and the scorned and the wounded, the lame
>   and the poor,

that Lindsay mentions, but also to the well-heeled and respectable, to and including John P. Altgeld, Esq. Accordingly he favored correction of those conditions and never quite understood the fury that his course aroused.

Altgeld was born in the village of Nieder Selters, in Nassau, South Germany on December 30, 1847, but was brought to this country at the age of three months. The family settled in the hamlet of Newville, near Mansfield, Ohio, where the elder Altgeld pursued his trade of wagonmaking, none too successfully, but well enough to keep his family fed, clothed and housed. Perhaps he could have done more for his children, but he seems to have had a peasant's prejudice against book-learning. The boy was allowed to attend school two summers before he was twelve, but then he had to go to work. At seventeen by his own efforts, clandestinely assisted by his mother, he managed to attend high school for awhile and at nineteen he became a schoolteacher himself, after service in the Union army lasting only a few months but long enough to give him a malarial infection from which he never fully recovered. At twenty-one he started west on an odyssey that brought him to Savannah, Missouri, ill and completely destitute; he was befriended by a farm family with whom he took service as a laborer, but within three years he had learned enough law to qualify for the bar and won enough friends to be elected county attorney in 1874.

But a year later he suddenly threw up the job, probably on account of a disappointment in love, according to Barnard, his biographer,* and departed for Chicago. There he hung out his shingle and for a year or two had very hard sledding, but then began to pick up practice through the aid of three singularly assorted friends, a prominent corporation lawyer, a labor leader and a professional gambler. From that point on he prospered. He made money at the bar, and presently he began to dabble in real estate, at which he made still more money. Within ten years he was a real-estate operator in a big way, was called a millionaire and was probably worth $250,000 which was as much money as he wanted. So he wrote a book on penology, went into politics, was elected Governor of Illinois in the Democratic sweep of 1892, and by his reforms and especially by his pardon of the men convicted of the Haymarket bombing brought down upon himself the fury of the conservatives, who defeated him in 1896, although he ran ahead of the national ticket. He died suddenly in 1902, still campaigning for a lost cause, this time Boer independence. Twenty years later Lindsay described the obsequies:

> They had snarled at you, barked at you, foamed at you, day
>   after day,
> Now you were ended. They praised you . . . and laid you
>   away.

More than fifty years later it is easy to see Altgeld as a highly civilized man with a keen sense of the realities. Except for Boer independence practically everything he advocated has long since been accepted; and until recent years, when the ugly stain of *apartheid* darkened the record, mil-

* Barnard, Harry, *Eagle Forgotten.*

lions of Americans clung to the belief that the destruction of the South African Republic represented a setback to civilization. So it is a temptation to explain the ordeal of Altgeld by his environment. What else could a civilized man expect at that time in that place?

> Hog Butcher for the World . . .
> Stormy, husky, brawling,
> City of the Big Shoulders,

as Carl Sandburg described it, the Chicago of sixty years ago was incurably romantic, which usually implies devotion to lies and cruelty. The conversion of a pestilential swamp into a tremendous city called for what Woodrow Wilson described, in another connection, as "force, force without stint or limit," and force was all that Chicago respected in those turbulent years, beginning with muscular power, but including cunning, ruthlessness and intellectual agility, which are all forms of force.

To the extent that force is represented by shrewdness and speed of mental operations, Altgeld had it, but it was at once his misfortune and his claim to fame that he had a good deal more. His success as a real-estate operator proves it. There is no evidence that his dealings were shady in the legal sense, or that he was noted for ruthlessness. He did not trample other members of the herd, he merely outran them; he perceived earlier than most the direction that development of the city was sure to take, and he got there first. Before the rest arrived he had two feet firmly planted in the trough.

But even then mere speculation in land did not satisfy him. Merely to acquire a piece of property, and then to sit inert until the rising tide of the city's population swept him effortlessly to a great profit was not enough; he felt an obligation to contribute something. Perhaps he had inherited from the old wagonmaker an instinctive desire to see something come from his own hand, so he developed from a mere speculator into a notable builder. In so doing he assumed additional risks, which eventually trapped him; but without doubt he also obtained satisfactions over and above the financial profits of his deals.

Perhaps, too, the fact that he was childless had some influence, as Barnard suggests. When his fortunes were at their nadir, back in Missouri, Altgeld fell in love with the daughter of the local magnate, but Father put his foot down heavily, and the romance was squelched; but when he began to come into his own the young lawyer went back and married the girl. It was a happy marriage, except for the lack of children, and this lack may have contributed to his desire to leave monumental structures behind him, since he could not leave living heirs.

Be that as it may, there was definitely nothing in this man's career up to the age of forty-five to mark him as a radical, or even as much of a humanitarian. He had, indeed, written a book whose tone is sufficiently indicated by its title: *Our Penal Machinery and Its Victims,* but a man who has practiced law in the criminal courts need not be much of a radical to perceive grave defects in the penal system. Altgeld may have been a little more emphatic than the average, but what he said was essentially what had been said by every writer on prison conditions since Daniel Defoe; at most it proved that he was realistic, not radical.

A friendly biographer describes him at the moment when he was inaugurated Governor, on January 10, 1893, as far indeed from the "bleeding heart" of the reactionaries' scorn. "Altgeld was a humanitarian whose heart ached over injustice," he concedes, then promptly adds, "but he was above all a human being—and a politician, loving the perquisites of political success, the sensation of being in the public eye, the acclaim, the prestige, and all the rest of it." *

The biographer is convinced that Altgeld went to the Governor's Mansion at Springfield looking upon it as merely a way-station on the road to the United States Senate. One of his associates, William H. Hinrichsen, elected with Altgeld as Secretary of State, expressed the opinion that had the Governor died at that moment "he would have had a place in the history of the state as no more than a lucky politician." Certainly in 1893 there was no reason to suspect that Altgeld would ever figure prominently as a member of the Lunatic Fringe.

But the outgoing Governor had unloaded upon his successor what was probably the most noisome stinker in American judicial history prior to the Sacco-Vanzetti case. This was the matter of the Haymarket anarchists, four of whom had been hanged, and three imprisoned for life for a bombing that nobody claimed they had committed. The argument was that they had inspired it and therefore were as guilty as the man who threw the bomb.

It had happened away back in 1886, when labor unions were just beginning to gain some real strength, and employers were terrified out of their wits. The police had shot and killed two strikers in a clash at a strike-bound plant and a meeting of protest had been called for a Chicago square called the Haymarket. A great deal of soap-box oratory had been discharged during the evening, but a storm began to threaten and most of the crowd drifted away. The mayor of Chicago, who had attended somewhat apprehensively, made up his mind that everything was going to be all right, and left. The man presiding was about to put a motion to adjourn when some two hundred and fifty police suddenly converged upon the crowd from the streets leading off the square.

* Barnard, Harry, *Eagle Forgotten,* p. 165.

In the momentary confusion that followed nobody knows exactly what happened. There were witnesses who swore that some policemen fired on the crowd, others who swore that they did not; but as the solid body of police marched upon the crowd someone, never identified, but certainly none of those on the platform, hurled a dynamite bomb into the platoon. The explosion killed one officer on the spot and six others died later of wounds. Then the police did fire. They kept up a fusillade for more than two minutes, killing one man certainly and wounding an unknown number—for, naturally, nobody was going to report a wound received at the Haymarket and risk being hanged as a rioter. Sixty-seven policemen reported for treatment, most of them with bullet wounds—a fact that led to the suspicion that in the confusion they shot each other.

Since the actual assassin had escaped, the police rounded up every known anarchist in the city and many of the prominent labor leaders. Most of them were later released, but eight were brought to trial on a first-degree murder charge. It was admitted that none of the eight threw the bomb, and only two of them had attended the meeting, but it was easy to prove that all of them had talked a lot of inflammatory nonsense, from which it was argued that they had incited the outrage and therefore were as guilty as the bomb-thrower. All were convicted, four were hanged, one committed suicide, and three were sent to the penitentiary for life.

Their trial was an astounding demonstration of the murderous proclivity of frightened respectability. It showed once more that while an out-and-out desperado, a Captain Kidd or an Attila, may eventually become sated with blood, a terrified Sunday-school superintendent or a highly moral attorney, a Robespierre, is never satisfied. The people responsible for the butchery of the Chicago anarchists were not the human garbage inhabiting Skid Row; they were the city's most respectable element, the inhabitants of the fashionable residential districts, the members of the most exclusive and expensive clubs, those who looked upon themselves as the upper classes.

From the standpoint of society the hanging of four anarchists of doubtful sanity and worse than doubtful moral worth was the lesser part of their offense; the gravamen of it was the murder of the law. As an example of the administration of justice the trial was a grisly farce. Judge Joseph Eaton Gary, who presided, was later portrayed by radicals as a monster comparable to the infamous Jeffreys of the Bloody Assizes, but he was nothing of the sort; he was merely a respectable poltroon. There is no reason to doubt that his fright was perfectly genuine, and fright so benumbed his wits that he was really unable to see that his conduct on the bench was making a travesty of the trial. Again and again when a prospective juror frankly admitted that he had formed *and expressed* the opinion that the accused were guilty and doubted that any evidence would change his opinion, the judge overruled the defense's challenge for cause and seated the man. He overruled the motion for separate trials. He overruled practically every motion the defense made. He all but convicted the defendants from the bench. Yet six years later he was so perfectly assured of his own righteousness that he wrote a magazine article reviewing the case in which he uttered not a word in defense of his own conduct, obviously unaware that it needed defense. He topped Samuel Sewall, who presided over the Salem witchcraft trials, for it took Sewall only five years to realize that he had been wrong and to confess it publicly. Sewall's cowardice was momentary, but Gary apparently never got over his fright.

Yet if he furnished a textbook case of an improper trial, the Supreme Court of Illinois capped it with an equally as-

tounding case of an improper review. Like the Supreme
Court of Massachusetts in the Sacco-Vanzetti case forty years
later, it resolved itself into a court of law, not a court of justice, and on technicalities, some of them extremely tenuous,
managed to uphold Judge Gary on every important point.
Indeed, in the matter of seating a juror who had not only
formed but publicly expressed an opinion adverse to the
defendants, it reversed its own ruling in a case only a year
or two earlier.

So August Spies, Adolph Fischer, George Engels and Albert
Parsons were hanged by the neck until they were dead. Louis
Lingg had committed suicide in prison, but Oscar Neebe,
against whom the state's attorney himself admitted that the
case was very poor, Samuel Felden and Michael Schwab were
still in Joliet penitentiary, serving life sentences when John
P. Altgeld was inaugurated as Governor.

Of course this had not passed without protest. Chicago
was not inhabited exclusively by Little Miss Muffets of both
sexes. It had its quota of full-grown men, capable of looking
even upon an anarchist spider without taking to panic flight,
and they expressed their horror and disgust in no uncertain
terms. Clarence Darrow was one of them and Louis Schilling,
the labor leader, was of course another; but they also included such figures as United States Senator Lyman Trumbull and Lyman J. Gage, president of the First National Bank
of Chicago. Scores of others who were certainly no friends
of anarchy added their voices to the protest.

Curiously, John P. Altgeld was not one of them. There is
no doubt where his sympathies lay, but he was running for
Governor, and to take either side in the dispute might easily
have defeated him. This cynicism—why try to evade the ugly
word?; a sense of practicality in politics does involve some
element of cynicism—is itself enough to demolish the notion

that this man was an impractical idealist. He knew what he wanted, he knew how to get it, and he believed, perhaps rightly, that his objective was more important than anything he could accomplish in behalf of the condemned men by joining publicly in the protest. So he said not a word in the red-hot period between the trial and the executions; he devoted his energies to his own campaign.

But once he was elected Governor the responsibility devolved upon him. Five of the men were dead, but three were still living and if the death sentences were wrong, so were the life sentences. The Governor, and the Governor alone, had power to rectify that part of the wrong, if he believed it was a wrong; and his refusal to act would be as decisive as acting.

Altgeld acted, but neither gladly nor thoughtlessly. Six months after his inauguration he pardoned all three; but in that six months he had studied the whole record carefully, and the document, running to 18,000 words, in which he explained his action is his testament to succeeding generations. Barnard, his biographer, plainly regards it as an unwise, if not a downright lunatic document from the standpoint of practical politics, and perhaps it is; nevertheless, there are elements of greatness in it.

Assuming that a pardon should have been issued, Altgeld had three possible explanations for such action, two of which might have been politically acceptable. One was that the verdict and the sentences that followed, however justifiable they may have been under the letter of the law, outraged the moral sensibilities of the people of Illinois, and ought to be set aside on that ground. To sustain him in that position he might have had a petition with certainly 50,000 and perhaps 100,000 signatures. Schilling was already busily engaged in preparing such a petition. The majority of the names would, of course, have represented working people, a good many of them socialists, and some, no doubt, anarchists; but it would also have borne such names as that of Goudy, the corporation lawyer, Lambert Tree, a highly respected judge, Potter Palmer, the millionaire capitalist, Marvin Hughitt, president of the Chicago & Northwestern Railroad, E. S. Dreyer, the private banker, and Lyman Gage, the national banker, Jane Addams and Henry Demarest Lloyd, the liberals, and Senator Trumbull.

He would have had, also, a sound legal position. Although this was a case in criminal law, he might have argued, very plausibly, that the basic principle of equity applied even here—that is, that the pardoning power is in criminal law what equity is in civil law, a means to provide a remedy where the law, by reason of its universality, might work injustice. If he had advanced such reasoning, even those who disagreed with it would have been reduced to arguing that the Governor was practicing bad law and the whole thing might have dissolved in an argument over technicalities.

If he disliked this, he had still the argument that the men had served six years for a crime that, by the admission of the state itself did not involve throwing a bomb, but only incitement to bomb-throwing. On the evidence they had not even incited the throwing of this particular bomb; in fact, the two who were on the spot argued against violence at that particular time. Therefore, they had been sent to prison not for any overt act, but for foolish and vicious talk, and six years for mere talk is a pretty stiff sentence.

Therefore the Governor might have argued that six years was enough, that substantive justice had been done, and the state of Illinois might reasonably show mercy to the survivors. If he had so argued, he would still have been denounced as a soft-headed sentimentalist, but hardly as anything worse. The whole thing might have dissolved in an argument over theories of crime and punishment.

But as Altgeld studied the record he was more and more convinced that the damnable element in this proceeding was neither the shock it administered to the sense of public decency, nor the savagery of the punishment inflicted on the individuals on trial, but the outrage perpetrated upon the most rudimentary principles of justice and truth. He soon lost interest in the individuals concerned. What did their guilt or innocence matter in face of the appalling fact, as he saw it, that the courts of Illinois had been guilty of a shocking perversion of their power in order to satiate the blood-lust of the mob? When Justice herself turns prostitute the crime is more heinous than anything that the wickedest man alive can perpetrate as an individual; and in Altgeld's view Justice in this case had been prostituted.

But for a man in public office to say anything of the kind is, to put it mildly, not diplomatic and Altgeld sweat blood before he could make up his mind to do it. Either of the first two solutions would certainly have saved the men, and might have saved his political career, but neither would have salved his conscience. He was Governor of Illinois, sworn to defend the constitution and execute the laws, and he found in this case a deadly assault upon both constitution and law. He believed that he had no recourse but to meet that assault head-on; and he did it.

His manner of doing it shocked even some of his friends. He excoriated the yellow cur who had presided over the trial, and thereby startled even such people as Jane Addams and Clarence Darrow. Such divinity doth hedge a judge that neither of them could quite countenance an attack on a wearer of the judicial robe, especially on one who in all else was quite acceptable, having, indeed, no fault except "a liver white as milk." They did not understand, as to this day a great many Americans do not understand, that courage is

the mudsill of every other judicial virtue, and that pusil-
lanimity in a judge is more dangerous to the social order than
the venality of Francis Bacon and the vindictiveness of
George Jeffreys combined.

But Altgeld understood it, and with white-hot logic he
cauterized every one of the thirty-eight fatal errors that Joseph Eaton Gary had perpetrated in the course of the trial.
Naturally, the unthinking, and even a great many sensible
people, assumed that he was less interested in freeing the
prisoners than he was in crucifying Judge Gary. In a sense,
they were right. Altgeld believed that in prostituting justice
the judge had committed a crime worse than the murder
with which the defendants were charged; and he said so—in
18,000 words.

Sixty years later an impartial observer must admit that this
enlisted him definitely in the Lunatic Fringe. Any public
official who gives rein to a passion for abstract justice in the
modern world is, as far as his private fortunes are concerned,
lunatic. Like the merchants of Tyre, he may be among "the
honorable of the earth," but among seekers of prosperity and
peace he is as crazy as the traditional bat.

In Altgeld's case they poured it on. Joseph Medill's Chicago *Tribune,* for instance, thenceforth habitually referred
to him as the "anarchist Governor"—that same *Tribune* that
a year earlier had offered as a solution for the plague of
tramps that unemployment had brought upon the country
the dainty suggestion that suburban housewives should give
each applicant at her door food liberally spiced with arsenic
or strychnine. The *Tribune* doubtless was being facetious;
but its misplaced humor left it in no position to criticize a
Governor for pardoning men convicted of incitement to
crime. It is, however, a very familiar story. Terrified respectability, committing every crime in the book, always de-
mands the blood of any others who may incite to crime.

Incitation to crime is exclusively the privilege of proper citizens—a Theodore Dwight, a "broadcloth mob" in Boston, a Joseph Medill, while a Jefferson, a Garrison, an Altgeld, for resisting the crimes of the "rich and well-born" becomes an anarchist.

Altgeld had expected denunciation. Indeed, he had said to Darrow that if he decided to pardon the anarchists, "Let me tell you, from that day I will be a dead man" politically. Even so, he was not prepared either for the fury or for the magnitude of the storm that burst upon him. A realist himself, he could not understand why the public was ignoring the real danger and concentrating upon a relatively trifling issue, namely, the fate of three individuals. Yet Altgeld had put it as plainly as words could express it: "No greater danger could possibly threaten our institutions than to have the courts of justice run wild, or give way to public clamor."

At least a third of Chicago, and by far the most articulate and loud-mouthed third, did not believe that for a moment. Probably a third of America, still articulate and still loud-mouthed, does not believe it to this day—hence such things as the Sacco-Vanzetti executions, lynch law, Ku Kluxism and McCarthyism. A third of Chicago in 1894 quite sincerely believed that national security lies, not in respect for the justice of the government, but in fear of the power of the government. These people felt—and the same kind of people still feel—that for the government to butcher the recalcitrant strengthened it. Altgeld, moved more by reason than by fear, knew that indiscriminate butchery inevitably weakens government by alienating reasonable people.

This was true. The pardon of the three anarchists undoubtedly strengthened respect for the state of Illinois among the masses and especially among the workers. This was amply demonstrated in the troubled times that followed. Economic depression lay heavily upon the land and a certain segment of employers—to do them justice, not all, or even a majority, but a group with power disproportionate to its numbers—conceived the idea of taking advantage of the depression to crush the rising power of labor. The result was an epidemic of strikes and lockouts, with the usual dismal accompaniment of murderous attacks upon labor by armed thugs hired for the purpose by the companies, and vicious attacks upon property by agitators driven insane by fanaticism.

In southern Illinois the situation was kept pretty well in hand by a very active Governor, who used troops constantly. This has been overlooked, or studiously ignored by many historians of the times, but the troop movements are on record and cannot be denied. Yet in that region not a single soldier was killed, nor did they kill anybody. The Governor was careful to investigate each case as it arose; he sent troops only when the threat of disorder was plain and plainly beyond control of the civil authorities. Once or twice he was deceived and sent troops when the real purpose was not to maintain law and order, but to break the strike. In every such case, however, as soon as he learned the truth he withdrew the troops. Labor soon discovered this and as a result paid high respect to the state troops; actual rioting in Southern Illinois was held to a minimum.

The big trouble broke in Chicago and the more one studies the record the plainer it becomes that not only was it the work of an *agent provocateur* but that the *agent* was none other than the government of the United States.

It began with a strike against the Pullman Company, manufacturers of palace cars for the railroads. George Pullman was an organizing genius who had made a colossal fortune in business, but in human relations he was a throwback from the nineteenth to the fourteenth century. He was a feudal lord, and it probably was not in him to be anything

else. He built a model village for his workers, green, pleasant and attractive—and charged them four times the rent
charged in the surrounding territory. He set up company
stores, company schools, company churches, which his em-
ployes had to visit. He boasted that the average wage he paid
was $1.87 a day, but he did not boast of the prices charged
in his company store. So he built up burning hatred in the
breasts of his men and was genuinely astonished when it
broke out. To all efforts to bring about arbitration of the
dispute over wages he had one stock reply: "There is nothing
to arbitrate."

This stiff-necked fool set back the orderly development of
labor-capital relations in this country for a full generation,
but there was nobody in authority in the city of Chicago or
in Cook County who would venture to oppose him. Neither
would they call on the Governor for help. Moreover, the
President in Washington was Grover Cleveland, who was
honest and bold, but had no more idea of the complexities
of the economic situation than he had of the theory of atomic
fission. He had appointed as his Attorney General a corporation lawyer, that is, a flunkey of Big Business, named
Richard Olney, and Olney burned to come to the rescue of
such an eminent representative of the Master Class as George
Pullman.

The railroad union had refused to handle Pullman cars on
any train manned by union men. They did not refuse to
handle any other trains, especially mail trains; but Olney
persuaded the President that the Pullman strike was holding
up the transmission of the United States mails. So, without
so much as a by-your-leave to the Governor of Illinois, the
President ordered Federal troops into Chicago, and the fat
was in the fire.

Rioting instantly broke out. Cars and buildings were
burned, and all railroad traffic, including mail trains, was

halted. The Federal troops, a thousand strong, moved one
train a distance of six blocks in one day.

Then, at last, the mayor of Chicago was persuaded to ask
the Governor for help. He instantly moved in state troops
and straightened out the situation in twenty-four hours. But
he also wrote two letters to the President of the United States
in which he told Grover Cleveland what he thought of him
and in no uncertain terms. He demanded removal of the
Federal troops, but he also made clear his resentment of being bypassed and in effect demanded an apology.

What he got was another storm of denunciation. As in
the case of the attack on Judge Gary he had fixed guilt where
it belonged instead of using some convenient scapegoat; and
the American public always resents having its illusions shattered.

Nevertheless in 1896 Altgeld, although he was defeated
for reelection got more votes in Illinois than Bryan could
win for the national Democratic ticket. He had established
a confidence in the state government that made its position
stronger than Washington's; and he had done it by nothing
more miraculous than exhibiting determination to enforce
the law against all classes alike.

It is startling to find how little evidence there is in the
record that Altgeld as Governor ever took one positive step
favorable to labor. He became the idol of labor not because
he did anything for it, but merely because he refused to employ the power of the state to crush it. He would not permit
the state troops to be used as strikebreakers. He would not
prostitute the courts into lackeys of employers' associations.
He would not tolerate conditions dangerous to public health
and safety merely because they were profitable to landlords
and employers; and for no more than this he became the
hero of the working class. This simple fact is the most stinging possible commentary on the social blindness of the time.

The legislation that he put through, regarded as radical then, almost all had to do with prevention of disease and accidents, that is to say, with elementary problems of public safety. Labor benefited, but only incidentally as labor shared in the general welfare. Only the most myopic vision could see class legislation in laws designed to eliminate firetraps and sweatshops that were fertile breeders of infectious disease.

After the defeat of 1896 there is little of public interest in the career of Altgeld. The sands were running out for him. The disease that had been an intermittent threat all his life now closed in and he died in 1902. But before his death he paid the penalty frequently exacted of a business man who is a constructive factor, rather than a mere speculator. He who builds anything, whether a railroad, an industry, or an office building, is always stalked by the hyenas who skulk in the shadows of the business world, who build nothing themselves, but watch vigilantly for any misstep by those who do build in order to snatch the fruits of their labor. In connection with his office building Altgeld had made a misstep in signing a contract with a predatory banker who took advantage of the depression to seize, by perfectly legal means, everything that Altgeld had. It was not theft; it was the kind of lawful operation that makes plain theft look positively virtuous by comparison. It was betrayal accompanied by protestations of friendship and a kiss. If he could have seen it, Judas Iscariot might have howled with laughter in hell.

But that is an old, familiar story without special significance for a generation living sixty years after. What is, or may be, significant is the combination of qualities that made John Peter Altgeld at once detested and adored and that has given him a prominent place among those whom Theodore

Roosevelt characterized as the Lunatic Fringe. Among them altruism was not dominant. Certainly, Altgeld was altruistic to a reasonable degree, but it is doubtful that he had in his veins more of the milk of human kindness than the ordinary decent citizen, than, say, Lyman Gage, the banker, or Potter Palmer, the merchant; as an altruist, he was not in the same class with Jane Addams, or Henry Demarest Lloyd.

Nor was he endowed with the stern, unbending virtue of Cato the Censor. As politicians go, Altgeld was definitely an honest man—but only as politicians go. Even Barnard, his friendly biographer, concedes that his intellectual integrity was not enough to prevent him from putting over some extremely dubious tricks in order to gain his point.

But one virtue he possessed in a supreme degree, to wit, courage. It was not fearlessness, which is often based on a stupid inability to see danger. It was that lordlier courage that holds a man to his duty even when he is desperately afraid. Altgeld was afraid to pardon the anarchists. He told Clarence Darrow that it was politically suicidal, and in a dozen other ways he showed that his very soul sickened within him when he thought of the inevitable consequences. But he did it, and in doing it an otherwise quite ordinary man rose to greatness. He was afraid to come into collision with the President of the United States, but he did that, too; and sealed his own political ruin by the very act that made him worthy of his office.

Altgeld's misfortune was his possession of—or his being possessed by—an intelligence so clear and keen that he could not blind himself to reality. To call him a friend of anarchy is nonsense; if the police had been able to lay hands on the man who threw the Haymarket bomb, Altgeld would have let him hang with never a twinge of conscience. But he knew that in making scapegoats of men who did not throw the bomb the state of Illinois was murdering the law, which he considered worse than killing policemen. He knew that in thrusting Federal troops into Chicago Grover Cleveland was inciting riot and bloodshed. Lacking the capacity that most of us have to draw before our eyes veils of pleasant illusion, he had to act, or know himself for a scoundrel.

He acted, and his action made him worthy of Lindsay's accolade, "O brave-hearted." More than that, his action has persisted as a vital spark in our politico-economic system something like the antibiotics that slowly spread through the blood-stream, destroying corruption and infection as they go; so perhaps he is also worthy of the poet's second apostrophe, "O wise man!" Anyhow, his memory persists while those of most of his opponents are forgotten; and to this day there are many who accept without question the romantic assertion with which the poem ends:

Sleep on, O brave-hearted, O wise man that kindled the flame—
To live in mankind is far more than to live in a name,
To live in mankind far, far more than to live in a name!

13

proem

The eccentrics studied in this volume are all people whose activities impinged upon the sphere of politics, even when their basic interest was not in the conduct of public affairs. Tom Paine and Henry George were more interested in ideas, and the Claflin sisters in personal advantage, than any of them were in governmental policies. But all of them had in some way an effect on political history; and all of them were, at most, eccentric, not mentally incompetent in the legal sense.

The vast army of fantastics in the realms of religion, morals and social customs could furnish material for many volumes; but not many of them have aroused any real alarm for the future of the republic and their successors today are not contributing much to the fear around us. However, now and then a moralist does have a measurable effect on politics, and now and then a member of the Lunatic Fringe has gone over the border line and has died in an insane asylum.

As illustrative of these points—and also, let it be admitted, for its sheer gaudiness, which could have been created only in the United States of America—there has been included in this collection the tale of:

CARRY NATION

who intimidated the strong boy

THEODORE ROOSEVELT was not a psychiatrist and when he spoke of the Lunatic Fringe he employed the words as a layman does. By a lunatic he did not mean a person so completely divorced from reality that his confinement in an institution is necessary for his own safety, as well as that of others. He meant odd characters who are, medically speaking, sane enough to be left at large and who may be intellectually brilliant.

Most of the subjects of this study have been revealed on examination as not merely sane, but in many cases saner than those of their contemporaries who derided them. But on rare occasions the course of American history has been perceptibly affected by persons whom the layman would describe as absolutely batty, and whom even medical men list as psychotic. John Randolph of Roanoke was one, and John Brown of Ossawattomie was almost certainly another. True, he was never certified, but he once disposed of a pair of captives by leisurely chopping small pieces off them with a cavalry sabre; and if that was the act of a sane man then all definitions are nonsense.

But of all people who have ended their days actually confined to a hospital for the mentally ill, none has had a political effect comparable to that produced by Carry Amelia Moore Nation, sometimes described as the scourge of Kansas, but in truth a visitation inflicted upon a Federal Union that had begged for it and richly deserved it.

Carry Nation was as definitely a product of American civilization as the skycraper, the movie, or the Constitution; but she was one of those products that the Rotary clubs pass over in discreet silence and that the chambers of commerce do not advertise; even the churches were abashed by her presence, as well they might be, and to this day social workers should look upon her, shudder, and beware.

For Carry was the bulldozer that cleared the way for the Anti-Saloon League juggernaut to roll to its incredible triumph over the prostrate, crushed forms of liberty, decency and reason. She was the woman who swept through the saloons of Kansas with a hatchet, destroying mirrors, bottles and mahogany bars amidst a mighty tumult, but also bringing crashing to the ground a towering social structure built by welding together hypocrisy, poltroonery, stupidity and greed. She was hated, feared, derided and deplored, not without reason, for she released upon us an era of insanity far surpassing the Salem witchcraft delusion. Yet now, nearly fifty years after her death, it is possible to believe that she was more than merely an affliction, that she was a catalyst. Perhaps Carry, or her equivalent, was the only means of precipitating the social irresponsibility held in solution in Americanism and inevitably poisoning the moral sense of Americans.

Carry Nation lived for sixty-five years, but only for something less than ten of them was she a national and, briefly, an international figure. She had attained a good deal of local notoriety earlier, but as a religious eccentric rather than as a social force, and the Kansas of that day was so full of religious eccentrics that one more or less made little difference. She was probably psychotic from an early age, but as one looks back upon it now the environment in which she lived seems to have been admirably adapted to mask and conceal any psychosis short of the most extreme types. In the vernacular, Carry was probably as crazy as a bat, but it hardly showed because at that she was not much nuttier than the society in which she lived.

She was born in central Kentucky in 1846, daughter of a planter and stock-dealer named Moore who was fairly prosperous in 1846 but was ruined by the Civil War. The family drifted down to Texas and back up to Belton, Missouri, where Moore settled in 1865. Thus the girl at nineteen was already living in poverty with galling memories of better days.

In later years officious perfectionists were always writing her name "Carrie" but that was wrong. In the family Bible, the only register of vital statistics known to Kentucky in those days, her father entered the fact of her birth under the name "Carry Amelia" which made it official, and none the less so because Moore may not have known how to spell.

He seems to have been fairly well-balanced mentally, although he lacked the force of character to make a comeback when war and a series of unlucky ventures had stripped him of his property. Perhaps he is not to be blamed, for he had a serious handicap in his wife; the lady developed the delusion that she was Queen Victoria, refusing to go out except in what she considered regal state, with outriders before her carriage and a footman in attendance. In the end she had to be committed to the state insane asylum and ended her days there. Her mother had been highly eccentric and a brother and a sister had died in asylums. Carry's mental heritage was dubious, to put it mildly.

Her girlhood was sickly. Forty years later she told audiences that she suffered from "consumption of the bowels" and was healed only by Divine interposition. The evidence is conclusive that she did suffer from a serious digestive disturbance, probably psychosomatic; which is no cause for wonder in view of the fact that from sixteen to nineteen hers was the life of a Displaced Person, driven from her home by war, making the long trek to Texas and back to Missouri, getting poorer with every day and dancing attendance on a madwoman.

At twenty-one she met and married the one man whom she ever really loved—or so he is described by Herbert Asbury, her sardonic but sympathetic biographer. This was a young physician with the unmelodious name of Gloyd, and the venture proved that even in love Carry was unlucky. Gloyd had served through the war and had come out with a whole skin, but with a fine case of alcoholism. Carry's family tried to prevent the match, but she could not be stopped, and it was misery from the beginning. Carry was convinced that alcoholism could be cured by argument, including public argument; as soon as Dr. Gloyd got a bit tight she poured on the invective, and when he fled she pursued him through the streets, driving him to take refuge in the Masonic lodge, which no woman was allowed to enter. The outcome was that he swiftly became a hopeless sot, and she became convinced that alcohol and fraternal orders were the ruin of the world. Just before her child was born her father came and took her back to his home; and after the birth of the child, a daughter, he refused to permit her to return. Six months later Dr. Gloyd was dead, probably of delirium tremens; he left no estate and his aged mother was destitute. Carry looked after her the rest of her life. The daughter, too, never was normal and grew up to be a dreadful burden, not a help.

So in her early twenties Carry became the breadwinner for an afflicted child and a senile mother-in-law, as well as attendant on a mentally irresponsible mother. Eventually she sought security in a loveless marriage to David Nation, nineteen years her senior, a preacher, a lawyer and a farmer and not much good at any of them. Nation failed at preaching, failed at farming, failed at the law, and Carry kept the family together by running boardinghouses in various towns where her ne'er-do-well husband tried various lines of endeavor. Eventually she was supporting six adults.

Yet it is impossible to say that it was all David Nation's fault. As a preacher, for example, he could hardly have been impressive with Carry sitting in a front pew, loudly correcting his pronunciation and, when she thought he had preached long enough, rising and saying, "David, that will be enough for today," and walking out. When her public career finally carried her away from him, he buckled down to the law and did rather well. He divorced Carry on the ground of desertion in 1901.

Hers was a hard life, full of misery, of grotesque comedy, and of backbreaking, bone-crushing labor; but no fair-minded reader of the story can deny that there was nobility in it. A woman who supported six helpless adults, two of them physically incapable of looking after themselves, had more than a touch of magnificence in her character. It is easy to believe that in a more favorable environment she might have developed superbly, becoming one of those great pioneer women whom the nation delights to honor; if, instead, she became a gargoyle, was it altogether her fault?

In any event, at about the age of forty-five she developed not so much a change of character as an extension of her interests. Up to that time her eccentricities had been confined for the most part to religious controversies that had led to her expulsion from two communions. But in the 'nineties, when she was running a hotel at Medicine Lodge, Kansas, she found in the Woman's Christian Temperance Union a new outlet for her energies. The W.C.T.U. was the sworn foe of alcohol and tobacco and to this program Carry Nation added her own violent distaste for fraternal orders, especially the Masons.

In her innumerable quarrels in innumerable churches she had already developed a considerable facility in public speaking; she had acquired an extraordinary vocabulary of invective, largely drawn from the Old Testament and touched with the sonority of the Hebrew Prophets in their more volcanic moods. This she put at the service of the W.C.T.U. which at first found it highly useful although Carry soon proceeded to lengths that began to embarrass the organization.

It was toward the turn of the century that, despairing of admonition and exhortation, she began to supplement them with direct action. One after another, she visited the illegal saloons in Medicine Lodge, first with a sackful of rocks, later with an iron bar, finally with a hatchet, and smashed the stock and fixtures. Little attention was paid to her activities, however, until she descended upon the city of Wichita, having given due notice of her intention, and swept through the bars there. Then at last the newspapers woke up; here was magnificent copy, and as Carry stalked from town to town she was attended by a platoon of reporters and later by a regiment of fanatical women.

She was arrested, of course. In all, she was arrested some thirty times and once spent seven weeks in jail, but her arrests were an embarrassment to the law because the saloons were in fact illegal. "You put me in here a cub," screamed Carry when she first landed in the pokey at Wichita, "but I will go out a roaring lion and I will make all hell howl." It was no idle threat, either; she made good on it.

Prohibition was embedded in the constitution of the state of Kansas, and the saloons were what the country later came to know as speakeasies, but in Kansas at that time they were

called joints by the populace and sample rooms by their proprietors. Carry could not be arrested for wrecking saloons
because the law could not admit that there were any saloons
in Kansas. A charge of malicious destruction of property
could not be made to stick when the property did not legally
exist. The usual charge, therefore, was disturbance of the
peace, a misdemeanor; and when Carry appeared in court
attended by a horde of maenads, often including some of
the most influential women in the community, it was a bold
magistrate who would even inflict a fine upon her. Usually
the case was dismissed, and when a fine was imposed it was
instantly paid by her enthusiastic followers.

Her publicity value was quickly recognized by shrewd
managers of lecture bureaus, who put her under contract and
carried her all over the country and eventually to the British
Isles. She visited Harvard and Yale, which she denounced as
"hell-holes" to the ironical cheers of the delighted students.
She drew large audiences everywhere and added to her fees
by the sale of miniature hatchets. Her income for a while
ran as high as $300 a week, which was big money fifty years
ago, and during her last years she was relieved of the necessity of hard physical drudgery. But the nervous strain took
its toll. She broke under it and retired to a farm she had
bought in the Ozark mountains; eventually she had to be
confined to a mental institution and died there in 1911.

In later years some observers, wise after the event, asserted
that Carry Nation could have been stopped in the beginning
by one courageous bartender with a bung-starter. But it is
safe to say that anyone who holds that view never saw Carry
in her heyday. She was a battle cruiser. She was nearly six
feet tall—a six-foot woman looks much bigger than a six-foot
man—and many years of scrubbing boardinghouse floors,
chopping wood, lugging heavy trays and scuttles of coal, and
bending over a wash tub had given her the arms and shoul-

ders of a stevedore. When she barged into John L. Sullivan's place in New York the heavyweight champion fled, and the Strong Boy was no mollycoddle. What wonder that the flaccid barkeeps of Kansas were scattered like chaff before a whirlwind!

More than that, her formidable muscular development was reinforced by a psychological power much more fearsome. From her youth up Carry Nation had been subject to mystic religious experiences that often amounted to seizures. Once as she was listening to a sermon in church she suddenly saw the preacher surrounded by a nimbus of more than earthly effulgence and felt the church, congregation and all, caught up into the clouds; so strong was the seizure that when it had passed she was astonished to note that other people had perceived nothing. But that did not shake her faith in the reality of the experience; it merely persuaded her that she was singled out for divine favor accorded to no one else.

To psychiatrists this is a familiar picture and they account for it readily enough without recourse to the supernatural; but even psychiatrists admit that the person so affected may draw from the experience a moral energy that is potent indeed. A six-foot woman armed with a hatchet and an absolute certainty that she is the chosen instrument of the Lord is too much for a bishop to handle, to say nothing of a wretched bartender aware that he is already on the wrong side of the law. This writer as a small boy saw Carry Nation on the platform; she was the very embodiment not only of all he had ever seen, but of all he had ever read in fairy tales or imagined in childish nightmares of ruthless stepmothers and formidable maiden aunts and powerful nursemaids and other family gorgons. She did not suggest a witch, for witches are in league with the Devil, and Carry was surrounded by an aura of inhuman, irresistible and remorseless righteousness. It has never entered the boy's mind in all the years that have followed to asperse the courage of the proprietors of the Kansas joints. They never had a chance.

It is of record that Carry was twice defeated, but never by men. Once, early in her career, she was horsewhipped by a mob of women; and on a later occasion she made the tactical blunder of joining single combat with a saloonkeeper's wife armed with a broom. Carry's hatchet was of no avail against Hebe's besom and she was chased down the street and off the field, to her intense chagrin.

On several occasions she was handled roughly both by mobs and by police; but in return she sent a number of officers to the police surgeon with dislocated joints and severe contusions. Once when a pint-sized sheriff attempted to take her into custody in a railway station she seized him by both ears and rushed him through the waiting-room shaking his head until his brains rattled. It took four city policemen to rescue him.

She soon became the nightmare of every jailer in the state, for within ten minutes of being thrust into a cell she could and did convert the best-conducted Bastille into a madhouse. She would instantly begin singing, praying, and launching the thunders of Sinai at the luckless turnkeys, all with the utmost force of her very powerful lungs. Upon a tankful of drunks, already on the verge of the heebie-jeebies, the effect may be more easily imagined than described. Often the street outside would be filled with frenzied women, kneeling in the roadway to the disruption of traffic, singing hymns, praying and pouring vituperation upon the warders. The demoralization was so complete that usually within half an hour the chief jailer would be on the telephone to the district attorney, to the judge, to the mayor, to anybody who might give him release from this affliction. The law got no change at all from Carry.

She had been in the grave eight years when the Eighteenth Amendment was ratified and it has been assumed in some quarters that she had nothing to do with it. But a sounder estimate is that of Kenneth M. Gould, who wrote the sketch of her in the *Dictionary of American Biography:* "A just appraisal of the social and psychological forces contributing to that end must certainly give her a large, if unpremeditated, place in the furthering of the program for forcible prohibition."

If that is true, her grotesque career cannot be relegated to collections of curiosa but has a legitimate place in serious history. Her unfortunate inheritance is not the sole explanation of Carry Nation; to a very large extent she was a product of the social conditions existing at her time, and this fact should not be ignored by anyone who holds that study of the past opens the way to a better understanding of the present and is the sole basis of an informed guess as to the future. The flat truth is that Carry Nation was as profoundly American as Abraham Lincoln. Neither could have arisen in any other environment. The fact that one is among the proudest ornaments of our civilization and the other among its defacements is irrelevant to their Americanism. It is important to know that our society has been well designed to produce monstrosities as well as magnificoes; for that leads to speculation on the extent to which it is still capable of such productions.

The true begetter of Carry Nation's public career was the hypocrisy of the law in Kansas—but a hypocrisy not confined to Kansas by a great deal. It was not merely the attitude of enforcement officials who winked at gross and flagrant violations. The original hypocrisy was the act of embedding sumptuary legislation in the organic law of a state ostensibly dedicated to democracy. The organic law, the constitution, of a state is the formal definition of the principles on which the government of that state proposes to operate; if one of those principles is that the will of the majority is to prevail in the ordinary conduct of public affairs, then the insertion of another clause that inhibits rule of the majority is hypocritical. Under the mask of democracy, it repudiates the vital principle of democracy, majority rule.

Temperance is a principle, but prohibition of the sale of alcoholic beverages is merely a policy designed to promote the principle. The error of the prohibitionists was that of attempting to erect their favored policy into an immortal principle by including it among the principles in the organic law. They were driven to this by a well-justified fear that in time the opinion of the majority might turn against their policy; so they endeavored to make it difficult or impossible for this adverse opinion to prevail.

It would be a serious error, though, to attribute this solely to the innate contumacy of the prohibitionists. If it was an untenable position, it was one to which they had been driven, not one they assumed by deliberate choice. At the turn of the century the liquor traffic in the United States was dominated by men whose insensate folly has rarely been matched in all the annals of human stupidity. If destruction finally came upon them, it was because they had long and insistently begged for it.

The saloon, the point of contact between the industry and the voting public, was of course the point that should have been most carefully guarded to prevent the development of ill-will. Instead, it was propelled, largely by brewers and distillers, into courses that could not have been better designed to propagate hatred and load the vials of wrath.

For one thing, respectable women were excluded from the saloon, not by formal regulation, but by the fact that most saloons were so offensive to the eye, the ear and the nostrils that women found them intolerable. Toward the end of the

era the typical saloonkeeper was no longer a business man
in his own right, with a stake in the community that gave
him a sense of social responsibility. He was merely a hireling
of some distillery or brewery that owned the premises and
could eject him at pleasure. His sole function was to push
his employer's product, and if he pushed it successfully he
could rely on his employer to defend him if he got into trouble with the law. The distilleries and breweries had money
enough and usually had influence enough to make the defense effective, and it became harder and harder to bring a
saloonkeeper to book even for flagrant offenses.

So regulation, even of the most reasonable kind, became
a mockery and a byword. Sales to minors, sales to men already beastly drunk, sales to confirmed alcoholics whose affliction was well known, were matters of course. Closing
hours were blandly ignored. This lawlessness tended to drive
reputable men out of the business and it was taken over by
lower and lower types who welcomed the patronage of sots,
prostitutes and criminals as long as they had money to spend.

Thus the saloon, once "the poor man's club," gradually
began to deserve the name of "hell-hole" that the prohibitionists applied to it. To cap it all, when the industry found
itself under increasingly heavy attack, its method of defense
was not to redress the genuine grievances of the public, but
to resort to corruption of public officials, bribery and vote-
buying in defiance of the most rudimentary decency.

The end was that the industry's ruthless contempt for the
processes of democracy inspired an equally ruthless contempt
in its enemies. Since it was being made to appear that the
will of the majority countenanced this outrage, the prohibitionists undertook to hobble the will of the majority by constitutional amendment. And they did it.

We understand this clearly since the error of Kansas in
1880 was repeated by the United States forty years later; but

it is not certain that we have attained even yet a clear comprehension of what it was that led to the error. It was the intellectual arrogance that assumes that we are as of this moment so irreproachably correct in our ideas that it is impossible for us to be wrong and that any who oppose us, either now or in the future, are necessarily motivated by evil desires.

This was certainly not clear to most of our people as late as 1951, for in that year once more we embodied a policy in the organic law and attempted to bind the majority to that policy throughout the future. This was in the adoption of the Twenty-Second Amendment, which forbids the majority to continue the same man in the office of President for more than ten years. It was arrogant and hypocritical in that it repudiated the principle of majority rule and arrogated to the men of 1951 the right to control policy through all coming generations. Their wisdom may have been great, but not that great. In the course of time it may plunge this nation into trouble even more serious than the saturnalia of the prohibition era.

It is, of course, an oversimplification to attribute Carry Nation's career entirely to her unfortunate experience with alcoholism. The total organization of society in her time contributed to the result. To some extent the evils under which she suffered have been corrected. The legal handicaps laid upon women by reason of their sex have been removed in large part, if not entirely. Today in most states, definitely in Kansas, society shows more consideration for victims of the social system. A widow struggling to support a family today can claim public assistance undreamed of when Dr. Gloyd lost his final bout with John Barleycorn. Today we admit in theory, although not too completely in practice, the responsibility of society to prevent the ruin of a whole family by the mental illness of one member. Today we are permitted to hope that the general advance of civilization has reduced somewhat the chance that a woman with some magnificent traits of character will be left alone to cope with "unmerciful disaster" until she becomes such a grotesque and frantic scourge as this one was.

Modern American society has abolished some of the conditions that produced Carry Nation, but that we are now immune to mania in case another such apparition should appear is by no means certain. The whirling dervish still exerts an irresistible fascination upon Americans and faith in panaceas is far from dead. The spectacular career of Senator McCarthy, belaboring the Communist spy as Carry Nation belabored Freemasonry, was not a phenomenon of the Edwardian age, yet for a time his success vastly exceeded hers. We are not yet a nation of philosophers, not by many a long Scotch mile.

The inclusion of Carry Nation in Theodore Roosevelt's Lunatic Fringe is justified by her function as a sort of moral and social vesicant. She was a blistering application that drew to a head the poisons generated in our political system by the doctrine that morality can be legislated into existence in a population that does not desire it. Her activity spurred the prohibition movement into frenzy. True, the frenzy brought it to a head that all but killed law and order throughout the country, but perhaps by no other method could we have been rid of it so soon.

She was not admirable, but she was a salutary warning. And in her role as an individual, not as a public terror, she was pitiable.

14

proem

The dominant theme of this book, thus far, has been the abundance of evidence that the fears excited by the Lunatic Fringe in the past have been grossly exaggerated. The passage of time has demonstrated that, more often than not, the apparitions that frightened us should have been welcomed with relief, for they were not in fact hobgoblins, but guides pointing the way out of our difficulties.

Yet while that has been the case more often than not, it would be a mistake to assume that there is never any peril in this element. Huey Long of Louisiana was nothing to view complacently. Neither is McCarthy of Wisconsin. To balance the record, then, it is essential to examine at least one wild man who did not seem to be wild merely because he was ahead of his time, but who was wild in very fact.

A number of names present themselves, going back as far as Aaron Burr, but one, in particular, presents not only the case of a really dangerous man, but also a clear and decidedly chilling example of progressive deterioration. It is a case in which it is easy to see both that the man was wild and also what made him wild; and the explanation of his degeneration offers a stern warning to democracy. It is a system that is admirably adapted to produce great men; but when its methods are perverted it can just as readily produce terrible men.

In witness whereof, now give attention to the tale of:

TOM WATSON

who could dish it out, but couldn't take it

THE DEPRESSION following the panic of 1893 produced wonders, signs and portents everywhere but its most lasting as well as its most spectacular effects appeared in the southeastern states. Here was tragedy in the grand manner, the ruin, not of an individual but of a whole society, the woeful degeneration of Attica into Boeotia.

The nature of the change can be indicated most simply and most vividly by mere recital of the names of men the South sent to Washington to attract national attention. Before 1860: Washington, Jefferson, Marshall, Madison, Jackson, Clay, Calhoun, Polk. After 1890: Tillman, Watson, Vardaman, Heflin, Blease, Long, Bilbo. To the modern generation the names of Heflin and Blease may have no more significance than that of Tiglath-pileser II, but even young men remember Bilbo, the Mississippian whose senatorial courtesy was of the type that permitted him to address a Jewish correspondent as "Dear Kyke." The others were of the same order—ruffians, not statesmen.

During the republic's first half-century the South was so far its most civilized region that at least two-thirds of the statecraft, brilliant beyond all precedent, that created the United States was of Southern origin. In political genius, indeed, the South not only led the rest of the Union, but it was among the leaders of all time. The triad of Jefferson, author of the Declaration of Independence, Madison, father of the Constitution, and Marshall, interpreter of both, for the combination of intellectual originality and intellectual power stood above all except a very few very great statesmen,

American or other; yet for half a century the South continued to produce successors whose achievements in the field of government were only slightly less brilliant. Calhoun, last of the South's great political theorists, may have been a warped genius, but in sheer intellectual ability he compares favorably with the best; and among men of action from Washington, who established the republic on the shores of the Atlantic, to Polk, who carried it to the Pacific, the outstanding successes were Southern.

The moral and intellectual collapse of so great a region is one of the most startling phenomena in our political history, especially as the fire of political genius was never utterly extinguished, even in the South's darkest moments. Its affliction may be compared to a splitting of the personality, but not to complete stupor. Alabama, for instance, was represented in the Senate simultaneously by Oscar W. Underwood and J. Thomas Heflin; and Mississippi successively by John Sharp Williams and Theodore Bilbo. Underwood was ponderous and dull, but he is said to have been the only man in history able to write a complete tariff bill without consulting a reference book, and he was emphatically a gentleman. As for genuine statecraft, Williams was a lightweight, but he was intelligent, witty and impeccably correct in his manners. Each offset, to some extent, the simian antics of his colleague; and how one state could offer preferment to both has never been satisfactorily explained.

Perhaps the best effort along that line is Woodward's study of the man who was christened Edward Thomas Watson, but who reversed his given names as the result of an early love affair. Its special merit is due to the author's understanding that "his story is also in many ways the tragedy of a class, and more especially the tragedy of a section." * To know exactly

* Woodward, C. Vann. *Tom Watson, Agrarian Rebel.* 1938. Preface.

why Tom Watson blew up does not explain all the others, for Watson was immeasurably superior to Blease and Bilbo intellectually, and probably to the rest of them morally. Nevertheless today almost the only thing remembered to his credit is that he got his name attached to an excellent watermelon.

Against that the world balances the dreadful record of the last ten or fifteen years of his life, when he was poisonously anti-Negro, anti-Catholic and anti-Semitic. This has outweighed and obliterated the preceding thirty years of intelligent, unremitting and largely disinterested labor for the common good. He is an outstanding demonstration of the aphorism that

> The evil that men do lives after them,
> The good is oft interred with their bones,

and it would be as foolish as futile to try to rehabilitate him as a martyr unjustly thrown to the lions by malignant fate.

Tom was nothing of the sort. Like the rest of the ruffianly crew to which he belonged, he was a moral failure, richly deserving the condemnation that posterity has visited upon him. But he is more interesting than most of his type, not only because he was more intelligent but also because in the beginning he was richly endowed with what Woodrow Wilson called "the generous energies" of the American people. Hence it is easier to trace through him, rather than through most others, the degeneration of a society.

The Watsons were upper-class Georgians. This is not to say that they belonged to the tiny group of the extremely wealthy that Thomas Nelson Page's febrile imagination tried to convert into typical Southern planters. In 1860, according to Woodward, Georgia had 118,000 families of whom less than a third owned slaves, while only 6,300 owned more than twenty. Tom Watson's father had forty-five Negroes and

1,300 acres, which put him in the topmost six per cent on the economic scale. His estate was rated at $55,000 at a time when the purchasing power of a dollar was at least three times what it is today. It is no great distortion to compare his position to that of a man worth $200,000 a hundred years later.

But this did not make him an aristocrat, and emphatically not one of the idle rich. He was a country squire who could, and when necessary did, plow as straight a furrow as any man on the place, and who regarded it as sinful to allow children to grow up in idleness. He was of the sturdy stock that had given the nation such leaders as Andrew Jackson, Henry Clay and John C. Calhoun, and that gave to the Confederacy such generals as Stonewall Jackson, Stuart, the Johnstons and the Hills.

This class was smashed by the Civil War, although not as completely as the smaller class of landowners who numbered their slaves by hundreds and their acres by tens of thousands. They came back faster, perhaps, as Toynbee suggests, because they had not so far to fall. Economically, indeed, they rebounded with startling success. Long before Tom Watson's death such names as Duke, Reynolds, Candler and Cannon, all drawn from this class, began to be compared with the names of Rockefeller, Astor and Vanderbilt as symbols of great wealth.

But the psychological damage was not so swiftly repaired. A characteristic of the culture of the Old South too often ignored was its structural solidity—more apparent than real since its economy rested on the quicksand of slavery, but in appearance very convincing. It was a hierarchy in which everyone had his place, but within his place everyone felt secure. Forty years later Watson, looking back upon it, wrote,

"It seems to me that there was neither feverish haste upon it nor vagrant leisure, fretful exactitude nor slipshod looseness, miserly gripping nor spendthrift waste. .... That old South-ern homestead was a little kingdom, a complete social and industrial organism, almost wholly sufficient unto itself, ask-ing less of the outer world than it gave. How sound, sane, healthy it appears, even now, when compared to certain phases of certain other systems!"

Invasion, conquest and ten years' occupation by an enemy army reduced this social system to rubble even more com-pletely fragmented than was the social system of Germany ten years after the surrender of 1945. Such conditions facil-itate the emergence of powerful individuals, but the rugged individual who comes to the top may be a great man or a great villain, a Masaryk or a Hitler, a preserver or a looter.

Both types appeared in the South between 1865 and 1900, to enlarge and complete the confusion initiated by a disas-trous war. In Georgia the state came to be dominated by a triumvirate made up of two Confederate generals, Alfred H. Colquitt and John B. Gordon and the Civil War Governor, Joseph E. Brown, and to this day controversy rages about these men. Colquitt and Gordon were popular heroes by reason of their excellent records—Gordon's was brilliant—in the Confederate army. Brown, the civilian, had been a pop-ular idol, but after the military occupation he favored sub-mission and ratification of the Fourteenth Amendment. He even affiliated briefly with the Republican party, which in-stantly changed him into a villain—a character that attached to Colquitt and Gordon in the eyes of many when the gen-erals joined forces with Brown.

Friendly historians have little difficulty in making out a case for these men as being realists who adopted the most sensible course for the rehabilitation of Georgia. It is highly probable that this is the light in which they saw themselves; but the damning fact remains that they all got rich in a devastated region. Twice in this century we have seen it demonstrated that the hyenas who prowl yesterday's battle-field can gorge themselves, so any man who becomes prosperous in a war-torn region has much to explain.

In any event, it is certain that Brown, Colquitt and Gordon were politicians, not sociologists, and their program of industrialization did nothing for the man at the bottom of the pile, the small farmer. With the coming of the great depression in the early nineties he was reduced to a level of existence at which he was worse fed, worse clothed, and worse housed than most of the slaves had been before the war.

Tom Watson adopted the cause of these people for reasons not hard to understand. He had dipped into that class himself. His father, twice wounded, came back from the war worse damaged psychologically than physically. With his labor force gone, his livestock destroyed, his fields weedgrown and the very fences ruined, his first move was to build a large and expensive mansion for his dwelling-house. This folly was followed by almost every other that a landowner could commit. By degrees he lost everything and before Tom had reached voting age the once upper-class family had sunk to the stratum of the poor whites.

A steady, relentless process of financial and social disintegration during one's formative years is enough to scar even a very tough personality. On a sensitive, redheaded youth, a romantic dreamer given to pouring out reams of florid poetry, the scarring effect must have been many times more severe. Tom Watson was basically an embittered man before he was twenty-one.

But he was far from crushed. Somehow he managed to get two years of college training, which he followed by two years of teaching, giving him money enough to study law. Once licensed, he specialized in criminal law, and the seething fury that the hard years had pent up within him was an asset in that kind of practice; it made him a tremendous advocate, before a jury well-nigh irresistible. Within a very few years his practice had grown so large that he was able to repurchase the old home and establish the family in it again.

But he did not forget the pit whence he was digged. He entered politics and in the state legislature became the voice of the Forgotten Man. For years the legislature had been the battleground of contending corporate interests and the intrusion of this raucous representative of "the wool-hat boys"—gentlemen of substance and standing wore silk hats—who had no money but a great many votes, was not welcomed. It became still more unwelcome when it became apparent that Watson's championship of the small farmers was building up a following increasing in numbers and whose devotion was rapidly mounting into fanaticism.

In 1890, as the candidate of the Farmers' Alliance, he easily won election to the national House of Representatives and then announced his adherence to the newly formed Populist party, becoming its candidate for Speaker and its recognized leader on the floor of the House. He fought for labor legislation and put through the first resolution for the rural free delivery of mails. In 1891 he founded the *People's Party Paper* which made him more or less the national spokesman for the movement.

Obviously, something had to be done, and the Democratic machine in Georgia acted ruthlessly. Watson's district was gerrymandered so successfully as to defeat him in 1892; but in the next two years his strength increased so tremendously that it was evident that he would win in spite of the gerrymander, so in one of the bloodiest and most shamelessly fraudulent elections in Georgia history they stole Tom Watson's seat and thought they had thrown him out of politics.

They had, indeed, as far as reputable statecraft is concerned. In 1896 the Populists indorsed Bryan for President, but nominated Watson for Vice President. He accepted the nomination, although he considered fusion a mistake, as, indeed, it proved to be. After the election he retired from public life, went to New York and devoted his time to writing and editing *Watson's Magazine,* devoted largely to Populism, but occasionally carrying contributions by such writers as Edwin Markham, Theodore Dreiser, Edgar Lee Masters and Maxim Gorky. Watson wrote the editorials in which he trumpeted Populist doctrine throughout the country with some effectiveness.

He also turned out a stream of books, of which a life of Napoleon was perhaps the best one-volume life in English up to that time. His biographies of Thomas Jefferson and Andrew Jackson stirred up some controversy but were too partisan to obtain wide acceptance. His one novel, *Bethany,* Woodward dismisses as a terrible novel, but as a genre-piece depicting the life of the Old South he believes that it takes high rank. Watson was essentially neither historian, biographer or novelist; he was a controversialist, and in that category he commands a very real respect.

After a few years a quarrel with his publisher sent him back to Georgia in 1907 where he established the *Weekly Jeffersonian,* and a monthly, *Watson's Jeffersonian Magazine.* But he did not return to Georgia intent on any literary achievement; he came on a mission of vengeance.

Apparently it was the election of 1894 that had done it. The machine in defiance of law, order, justice and every other form of decency had broken Watson's career; but in so doing they had converted a mildly radical reformer into a monster of what afterward came to be known as fascism. For years Watson made no attempt to run for office, but he sedulously organized his following, whipping it to frenzy by playing to every base passion, and then in elections hurling it against one after another of his betrayers. Man by man, he smashed them, he ground them to powder. In the process he very nearly smashed Georgia, dragging its public morality to a level that would have shamed Albania, and actually undermining the safety of life and property.

His cynicism became so complete that it passed beyond the ordinary definition of the term. The author of the life of Napoleon was a highly intelligent man who had read widely in European as well as American history; it is possible that he was even then somewhat prejudiced in favor of the Protestant and Aryan point of view, but it is flatly impossible to believe that he had anything but contempt for the crass and stupid lies propagated by the rabble of anti-Catholics and anti-Semites.

But by the early years of the present century his moral disintegration had proceeded so far that intellectual disintegration accompanied it. It is conceivable that he actually believed the loathsome stuff that he poured into his paper and his magazine; and cynicism is hardly the term for that state of mind. We have, in fact, no word for a man so corroded by intense and long-nurtured hatred that he has become the antithesis of what he once was; yet the phenomenon is by no means unfamiliar.

The most notorious incident of this phase of Watson's career occurred in 1915. Two years earlier a man of good family and some wealth was arrested and charged with the murder of a girl under circumstances so revolting that the crime seemed clearly the work of a pervert. The suspect was a Jew named Leo Frank; and while the police certainly had some reason other than religious prejudice for their action, from the moment of the arrest the effect of Watson's long campaign of fomenting prejudice became frightfully apparent. It was clear from the start that the accused was convicted before a single talesman had entered the jury-box, and with every step the subsequent proceedings became a more and more blatant travesty of a trial.

Curiously enough, Watson was silent until the verdict was returned. He seems to have been still enough of a lawyer to feel some uneasiness about making a direct, frontal attack on the judicial process. But he had done enough. His devoted followers rushed in with a clamor that shocked the nation. The day the jury took the case the courthouse was surrounded by a mob whose roar was clearly audible; and grave citizens begged the judge not to receive the verdict in Atlanta because an acquittal would certainly result in rioting and bloodshed.

Of course Tom Watson was not the creator of this horror. There was latent anti-Semitism in Georgia before he ever raised his voice; he merely nurtured it, as he nurtured anti-Catholicism and anti-Negroism. His damnation is not that he planted the seed, but that he fostered the poisonous growth, and when it became clear what he had done he had not the grace to stand appalled, as even Iscariot did. On the contrary, once the verdict had been returned and the defense took an appeal, he placed himself at the head of the pack, and with his genius for invective he outdid all others in pouring anathemas upon all who questioned the fairness of the trial.

The most disheartening phase of the whole affair was that the higher court in Georgia, as in Massachusetts when the Sacco-Vanzetti case came up a few years later, turned itself into a court of law, rather than a court of justice. Hiding behind technicalities it refused to upset a monstrously unfair proceeding, and the verdict stood approved. Then the whole storm burst upon the luckless Governor of Georgia with an aroused country demanding a commutation of the sentence and raving mobs threatening death to any official who should grant it.

John M. Slaton was certainly none of the world's great heroes, but he stands head and shoulders above the rest of

Georgia officialdom, for he had a way out and disdained to take it. The execution was set for the day after his term ended; but the responsibility was Slaton's, for the incoming Governor was bound hand and foot to Tom Watson and would certainly not lift a hand in Frank's favor. On the last day of his term Slaton commuted the sentence to life imprisonment.

It ended his political career and it came close to ending his life. Only a military guard enabled him to escape from Atlanta, and the mob went for him with such fury that sixteen soldiers were injured while protecting him. But he is the only Georgia official who came out of the affair with any shreds of manhood left.

Tom Watson's comment on the Governor's act in saving the man's life was, "We have been betrayed! The breath of some leprous monster has passed over us, and we feel like crying out, in horror and despair, 'Unclean! UNCLEAN!' " A short time later a fellow convict made a murderous attack on Frank, and while he was recovering a mob dragged him from the prison hospital and butchered him. Slaton's sacrifice was unavailing, as far as Frank was concerned, but it did serve notice on the world that there were some civilized men left in Georgia.

The remainder of Watson's career can be summarized briefly. The entry of the United States into the First World War soon gave him the most wonderful opportunity he had ever had to play upon ignorance, prejudice, cowardice and every other base passion. His publications became so outrageously seditious that they were barred from the mails and in Germany their author would have been hanged. But the American Cataline was elected to the United States Senate in 1920, where he spent his time pouring vituperation on Woodrow Wilson and the League of Nations until death cleansed the Senate of his presence in 1922.

Thirty years later this revolting story has one contemporary value and only one—it is a warning to all adherents of
democracy that they can, by their own folly, reproduce in
America the tragedy of Alcibiades in Athens. No doubt the
brilliant man who is embittered by injustice is from the beginning a flawed character; no doubt an Aristides, ostracized
for being just, emerges from the experience all the stronger;
but it is equally beyond doubt that an Alcibiades and a Tom
Watson can't take it, and by their very brilliance, once they
are driven into subversion, they become frightful dangers
to any democracy.

The thing most worth remembering about Tom Watson
—and about Heflin, Huey Long and, to some extent, even
Bilbo—is that he began as a genuine idealist, with great confidence in the processes of democracy, with sympathy for
those whom the imperfections of the system deprived of
equality of opportunity, and with a conviction that the primary function of statecraft is to correct the imperfections
and to bring the system to an ever closer approximation of
equal justice. But they were all, with the exception of Long,
completely humorless fellows with an exaggerated sense of
their own importance in the scheme of things; so when they
found themselves victims of strongly entrenched injustice,
they were unable to laugh it off and continue the fight along
the same lines, as greater men could—a Lincoln, for instance,
or a Gallatin, or even a Tilden.

It is with perfect justice that such characters are held up
as the reproach of democracy, for they are among its products. The faults and failings of a Hamilton, a Gouverneur
Morris, a John Randolph are not chargeable to democracy,
for they never had any real belief in the system, considering
aristocracy vastly preferable; nor are the Utopians, a Robert
Dale Owen, a Brigham Young, a Eugene Debs in any real
sense to be considered failures of American democracy, since

they considered one of its bases, a capitalistic economy, hopelessly unsound.

The open opposition of such men has never seriously threatened the continued existence of the republic; and the greatest of the group, Hamilton, added to its strength because he bent his genius to the task of making it work even though he doubted that it would survive long. It is the disillusioned and despairing that are the menace for the simple reason that all men are capable of disillusionment and despair, including millions who could never be converted to aristocratic or monarchical principles. No communist leader has ever collected enough American followers to elect a single avowed party member to Congress; but if John Steinbeck's Okies ever found a leader, this republic would be shaken to its foundations. They very nearly found one in Huey Long, and as realistic a politician as James A. Farley was appalled when a secret public-opinion poll revealed the number and the wide distribution of the Louisiana dictator's supporters.*

The question then arises immediately, what is it that makes a disappointed liberal so virulently poisonous? Probably it is a psychological defect that exists in us all, but that in many men is, if not cured, at least glossed over by humor. This is an inability to understand that democracy is none the less real for being more hypothetical than factual. So, for that matter, is civilization. No nation has ever been completely democratic, as none has ever been completely civilized. Nevertheless democracy and civilization both exist as ideals toward whose realization the best and wisest men have struggled throughout history. Nearly all men, except the completely irrational, realize this as regards civilization, and, knowing that it is a thin crust over the quagmire of barbarism, are not permanently unbalanced when the crust breaks

* See Farley, James A., *Behind the Ballots*, pp. 249-250.

through and war engulfs the world.

But the same attitude toward democracy is by no means as common. Without doubt we have boasted too much of our achievement. We permit schoolboys to be indoctrinated with the notion that we established freedom and equality in 1776; and some of them, when they find freedom and equality still missing in large areas of life nearly two hundred years after the Declaration of Independence, assume that they have been the victims of a monstrous fraud. In a way they have, but the fraud was perpetrated in the schoolroom, not in Independence Hall in Philadelphia. The men there present merely made an assertion of what was not a fact, what everybody knew was not a fact, and what it took seven years of war to establish as a fact, namely, "That these United Colonies are, and of right ought to be, free and independent states." Equally hypothetical was the assertion that "all men are created equal and endowed by their Creator with certain inalienable rights." That such an assertion would stand unsupported they did not imagine for an instant; which is why they ended by pledging to its support their lives, their fortunes and their sacred honor.

But to live on a tentative basis and to admit that our whole political system is a status, not of being but of becoming, requires a philosophical and psychological balance that not all men are capable of maintaining. Some turn reactionary and wear their lives out in a hopeless battle against any and every kind of change; others turn radical, and wear out their lives in the effort to speed up the process faster than the nature of things will allow. Both fight hopeless battles, yet each may achieve some measure of success and each in a different way may contribute to the development of civilization.

The dreadful case is that of the man who, starting with high hopes and generous impulses, allows repeated defeats to convince him of the rottenness of the system and the total depravity of his fellows. Then the energy and ability that might have made him great combine to make him monstrous. When conditions are exactly right he becomes a Hitler, and when they are only partially right he becomes a Tom Watson. The sinister factor in the situation is that conditions are always right to some extent in a democratic society.

For freedom is dangerous, as nobody knew better than the men who won freedom for this country. One has only to read Madison's notes on the Constitutional Convention to see how fear of the demagogue harried the Founding Fathers almost to the extent of becoming an obsession; and in Washington's Farewell Address there is a passage—written, presumably, by Hamilton but adopted by the President—portraying with prophetic insight the rise of such a man as Huey Long. It is true that neither Long nor anyone like him has attained the full extent of power feared by Washington, but the thing was possible then, is possible now, and as long as men remain free will remain possible.

Yet it was Franklin's opinion that any man who would abandon essential liberty to obtain temporary safety deserves neither liberty nor safety—and the events of this century have demonstrated that he will not long enjoy either. The idea that safety can be attained by putting down honest protest is fallacious, as most rational men agree. Where the split comes is on the proposition that no one except the protestant himself knows that a protest is dishonest. Yet it is true.

The inevitable inference is that the forcible suppression of any protest is wrong in a democratic society. One of the penalties of that wrong is the release upon society of a Tom Watson, a man of ability converted into a scourge. It is an appalling affliction; yet if it is an affliction caused by crushing a man by *force majeure* it is one that is richly deserved.

15

CONCLUSION

indorsing a philosopher, a pope and a poet

AT THE BEGINNING of the winter of 1956-57 the business of commenting on the state of the nation became an extra-hazardous occupation. Events were moving at such a tremendous pace that before comment could be transferred from the typewriter to the printed page it was easily possible that it might be invalidated and turned to derision by some totally unexpected upheaval, perhaps in a far corner of the world.

Between the writing and the publication of a book some months must elapse. As 1956 drew to a close, thunder on the left was rising from a mutter to a rumble, and the trembling augurs dared not predict that it would subside instead of mounting into a roar that would encompass the world.

The thunder was the hammering of the guns in Algeria, in Hungary, around the Suez Canal. They were far away, but their menace could not be ignored, for they were a threat to everything American down to and including a book of this kind, able to affect strongly its meaning and its purpose.

For if this book were to appear while the citizens of this republic were engaged in a red-hot, shooting war one of its principal theses would be rendered irrelevant, making the work in part aimless. This is the thesis that Americans in times of relative peace need, or certainly can use handily, some reassurance as to the future of the republic. As late as midsummer, 1956, this was incontestably true, for the air was filled with lamentations and dire predictions. Some of them undoubtedly were fraudulent, for a Presidential campaign was raging and during such occurrences the manufacture of hobgoblins always becomes a leading industry; but many of them were real in the sense that the Jeremiahs actually believed their own bunk. The book was planned and produced on the assumption that this atmosphere will still pervail on its publication date.

But if war breaks out it will be a different kind of country, unless all the records of the past are misleading. If war breaks out, the remainder of this chapter will have little more application to the United States of America than to the Tadzhik Soviet Socialist Republic in the fastnesses of Central Asia. For it is characteristic of the American that once he is confronted by a bad man with a gun, by an enemy that he can see and identify, the American becomes grimly confident and briskly efficient. In such circumstances he needs no reassurance and the labor of these pages is in vain. When the American knows that he runs some risk of getting his head knocked off by a cannon-ball he is imperturbable; it is when he fears that he may have his head turned by the siren songs of characters that he classifies vaguely as "subversives" that he falls into blind panic, stampedes, and tramples underfoot the guarantees of his own liberty and even of his physical safety.

But to withhold this comment until there is a reasonable certainty that it will still be apposite six months, or three months after it is written is impractical, for there has not been a day in seventeen years when there was a reasonable assurance that the United States would be even technically at peace six months later. The utmost that a contemporary writer can do is accompany his suggestions with an acknowl-

edgment that events may render them quite useless over-
night. Hence these lines.

There is a chance, however, that the Day of Armageddon
may be postponed yet a little while, and there is a moral certainty that the Day will pass. For peace is inevitable. That
is guaranteed by the fact that the strength of men is not inexhaustible; perhaps it is as true of modern men as of those
whom Calgacus denounced that "to plunder, to slaughter,
to steal, these things they misname empire; and where they
make a desert, they call it peace." Nevertheless peace always
returns; and it will return to this earth, even if it finds the
terrestrial globe only a cosmic cinder simmering with radio-
activity.

So "in time of war prepare for peace" would seem to be
an apothegm as sound as its converse, yet it has rarely been
seriously applied by the American people. Warning after
warning we have blithely disregarded. Salem, in 1692, should
have been a sufficient warning against all witch-hunts; since
it was not, the Reconstruction orgy after the Civil War
should have been a warning that witch-hunts may be political as well as religious; since it was not, the Mitchell Palmer
delusion in 1920 served notice that they may be ideological,
as well as political; but all of them did not prepare us, in
the middle of the twentieth century, to realize that patriotism
may degenerate into horrible fanaticism as readily as Calvinism did more than three hundred years ago.

Preparing for peace involves, first, accepting emotionally
as well as rationally—in bone and blood as well as in mind—
the fundamental truth that peace is not static; and, second,
cultivating sedulously the ability to contemplate the necessity of taking the next step, not with terror, but with the cool
calculation of an engineer figuring the size of the girders that
his bridge will require.

There is no impressive evidence—at least none visible to the naked eye—that Americans of this generation are making any effective effort to establish preparation for peace as part of the educational system. The perceptible effort is all the other way. The very first principle of any rational approach to the subject, the realization that peace is not static, seems to be intolerable to most of the self-appointed regulators of our schools; they regard any suggestion of change, in economics, in politics, or in social attitudes as a disturbance of the peace, not as part of its normal processes. Hence the present scornful rejection and the occasional persecution of the proponent of any new idea; hence the past inclusion in the Lunatic Fringe of men and women who were proposing what a later generation sees as the most obviously necessary change.

There is, of course, nothing specifically American in this. It is a human failing. It was shared by the Dicastery at Athens that judged Socrates and the Sanhedrin at Jerusalem that judged Christ; it was, in fact, even more conspicuous in them than it was in those Americans who adjudged Robert Oppenheimer unworthy of trust because he hesitated to advocate scientific experimentation that, as we know now, tends to poison the air that all living creatures breathe.

But *tu quoque* is not a logical argument, it is a fallacy, so listed by every elementary textbook. The impulse to murder is likewise common to all mankind, but that is no excuse for a civilized man to give way to it, much less to cultivate it; and the higher his standing on the scale of civilization, the more heinous his offense if he commits murder. The legal penalty is the same for all, but most men would regard a homicidal bishop with deeper horror than they felt for any of Al Capone's gunsels.

It happens that the American republic at this moment in history stands on a very high level of civilization. We may

be worthy of it, or we may not; that is immaterial to the argument. Not of our choice, and less by our own efforts than
by the inexorable march of events we have been thrust into
the leadership of the free nations. If, as we have proclaimed,
free men are peaceable men, it follows that this nation ought
to be conspicuously well prepared for carrying on peace—
better prepared for that than for carrying on war.

It is hard to understand how any candid man can seriously
maintain that we have measured up to our responsibility in
that respect. Certainly we talk about peace, world without
end. It is doubtful that history ever saw another nation so
completely infested with peace societies, foundations for
peace, papers and magazines for peace, lecturers for peace,
actors, singers, dancers and, I dare say, prize fighters and bar-
room bouncers, organized for peace and all giving tongue in
such a way as to make Bugle Ann seem a mere stuttering
amateur. Unfortunately, while a saving remnant of this mot-
ley array may speak with the voice of philosophy by far the
larger part of the noise resembles rather the voice of *Alouatta
ursina,* the howling monkey.

But there is a wide gap between talking about peace and
preparing for it. Preparing for peace means cultivating a
public opinion that will support the government in a program of action befitting the nation that holds leadership of
the peace-loving peoples of the world. Effort in this field is
certainly not conspicuous. One wing of the peace-mongers,
in so far as it contemplates action at all, advocates throwing
down our arms in the presence of heavily armed antagonists,
which is surrender, not struggle; and others apparently put
more trust in compacts among governments than in creation
of an electorate adequately informed of the conditions necessary to the maintenance of peace.

One of these conditions is certainly a reasonable hospitality to ideas. There is no lack of historical examples of the

folly of the opposite course. Toynbee offers twenty-one, and before more than a handful of Americans had ever heard of Toynbee one example had passed into popular speech in this country. The verb "to chinafy" was used by Theodore Roosevelt; it meant to adhere to a policy of intellectual, moral and spiritual, as well as political isolation, as imperial China did for centuries, with results that horrified Americans.

But while we accept the progression of human thought in theory, we are slow to apply the theory in practice. A fair statement of our actual position was made by a high government official, Secretary of the Air Force Quarles, speaking to a group of educators late in 1956. He said, "When we consider the great potential danger which our country faces and, as far as we can see, must continue to face, I think we are justified in placing something like wartime emphasis on our technological, as distinguished from our cultural, needs."

There is every reason to believe that Secretary Quarles voiced the dominant sentiment of the country. Probably he spoke for the majority. Certainly he spoke for a large and very influential minority, a group so strong that it has controlled high policy since the end of the Korean war.

For that reason the statement deserves more careful analysis than the unshared opinion of any one man can command. If it is a fact that the country favors, not merely now but for the predictable future, allowing potential—not clear and present, but potential—dangers to thrust technology ahead of culture as the chief concern of education, it can hardly be argued that we are preparing for peace, since the inclination of peace is not toward avoiding potential dangers, but toward improving potential opportunities.

It is also questionable that technology is the best defense against potential dangers. Against clear and present dangers, sharply defined and unmistakable, yes, technology must be our main reliance; but against potential dangers, not yet clearly defined but merely taking shape—that is, against the thing that may happen, not the one that must happen—the usefulness of technology is limited.

For the highest of all high explosives is not the hydrogen bomb, it is the human mind, as Russia discovered in Hungary in the autumn of 1956. To remove the detonator from this explosive, technology is a clumsy instrument; for this purpose what the bomb-squad needs is not physics, but psychology, not knowledge of the structure of the atom, but profound knowledge of the nature of man.

Hence the first preoccupation of the leader of the forces of peace must be to keep not bombs, but people from exploding; and the most efficient means of attaining that end is to imbue them with hope of better things to come. A man reasonably sure that tomorrow will bring an improvement is not likely to resort to violence today. He has too much to lose. It is when, in the words of the Communist Manifesto, you have nothing to lose but your chains, that you resort to the barricades and attempt to fight tanks by hurling paving-stones.

But the flame of hope is kept burning by one means only, namely, by feeding the flame with a constant flow of new ideas. It flickers and soon expires when the only fuel supplied it is sodden old straw.

Obviously, then, the way for any nation to prepare for peace is to convince the world, and first of all its own people, that it is receptive to the point of view of those who are dissatisfied with existing conditions and who can envisage an order of things that comes closer to the heart's desire. The fact that most of them are sure to be wrong, and that a certain proportion are likely to be downright insane, is irrelevant; the important point is that some of them are sure to be right and the maintenance of peace depends upon seizing and applying those ideas that are right even though they run contrary to prevailing opinion.

The point of view represented by Secretary Quarles is in line with this as far as the physical world is concerned. No group of men has been more hospitable to new ideas in their own line than American technologists; the proof is the prodigious technical achievement of the American economy; our productive capacity is the marvel of the modern world and the model even for our bitterest antagonists, who copy our methods and admit it, in fact, boast of it.

But the leadership we are called on to exercise in the immediate future and probably through the remainder of this century is not technical, it is political. To put it mildly, it seems less than wise, then, to devote our energies with wartime concentration to strengthening our technical position, which is already strong, to the neglect of our political position, which is precarious in the extreme. The weak point is the one to reinforce, if our whole position is to be made secure.

A leader who doesn't lead cannot retain his position. But political like any other leadership, is dependent upon alertness, resourcefulness and ingenuity, that is, upon the constant generation of new ideas in the specific field. Hostility to new ideas presages the decay of leadership. In recent years there has been much talk of the "flight from intelligence" in this country, but it is an abuse of the term. It is in reality a flight from novelty, which is consistent with a high level of intellectuality. John Adams, John C. Calhoun and William H. Taft were intelligent men, among the most intelligent this country ever produced; but their inability to adjust to new political ideas made their political leadership disastrous.

None of them, however, did much damage except to his own party and, in lesser degree, to his own country. None of them was in position to do more. But a mistake by an American political leader today will react not on the United States alone, but on every nation in the world. That is the penalty of leadership. Furthermore, since the selection of American leaders rests with the people, a public opinion hostile to every novel suggestion will inevitably result in the selection of leaders prone to political error.

There is no escaping the truth that when fear of taking the next step is rife among the people, the nation will hang back, even under the most competent leadership; and it is unlikely to have competent leadership for long. The problem is not that of choosing the right President; it is that of creating the right climate of opinion, which involves millions of voters.

"I have but one lamp by which my feet are guided and that is the lamp of experience," said Patrick Henry. "I know of no way of judging the future but by the past."

He spoke the words as a warning, but sometimes there is comfort in them. They should be taken to heart by any American whose courage begins to fail as he contemplates the confusion of fads and fancies, of isms and ologies that in the consulship of Plancus were unknown. Whether *consule Planco* to you means the days of Woodrow Wilson, or those of F. D. R., the principle is the same. We are beyond the point at which the wisdom of those men will suffice.

The temptation is to say, "Oh, no doubt they had their perplexities, but no earlier generation has had to contend with such lunatics as *our* lunatics." But if we say so, we flatter ourselves; they all looked just as bad as the worst before our eyes. Yet the baker's dozen that we have examined had all some intimation of the shape of things to come, some suggestion to offer which, if it had been adopted and adapted by more practical minds, might have delivered us from many

of the tribulations through which we have come. If they did
no more they at least defied and somewhat weakened the
"tyranny of opinion" that John Stuart Mill hated and feared;
and in that they are a lamp to our feet and a light to our
path.

For the tyranny of opinion can be endured by a free nation no more than the tyranny of George III, and the first
step toward throwing it off is to follow the advice of sardonic
Pope Julius: "Learn, my son, with what little wisdom the
world is governed."

If this process happens to be highly entertaining, surely
that is no objection. Rather, it is a merit when the current
tyranny of opinion is the tyranny of fear. The colossal gro-
tesquerie, the majestic buffoonery that punctuates American
history may be an offense to the prim, but to the ribald it
is a constant delight that makes their lives more worth living.
So they cherish not only the modicum of wisdom that the
Lunatic Fringe presented but also its indubitable lunacies.
At least they startle us out of lethargy, they make us more
vibrantly alive.

The Stentor of the Illinois prairies phrased it well. Vachel
Lindsay may not be the best of American poets, but he has
a strong claim to be considered the loudest; and he is a handy
bard to have around when the singer's voice must contend
against the artillery that is yelling across the sea. Hear him:

> There are plenty of sweeping, swinging, stinging, gor-
>   geous things to shout about,
> And knock your old blue devils out.

Among the "sweeping, swinging, stinging, georgeous
things," the Lunatic Fringe of the past is certainly to be
counted; and if of the past, why not of the present? To shout
is pleasanter than to shiver; and to shout rather than to
shiver at the appearance of a novel idea has the additional

advantage that it cannot be a complete mistake. Even if the idea is a bad one, the shout is still partially justified, for the evidence that someone still thinks, and still says what he thinks regardless of prevailing opinion is ample excuse for jubilation.

THE END